To: Mary

Hope this book is A blessing to you! You Are A blessing to me!

[illegible signature]

MORE THAN A CONQUEROR

Conquering Your Past

MIKE BENSON

WestBow Press books may be ordered through booksellers or by contacting:

WestBow Press
A Division of Thomas Nelson & Zondervan
1663 Liberty Drive
Bloomington, IN 47403
www.westbowpress.com
1 (866) 928-1240

ISBN: 978-1-5127-0598-0 (sc)
ISBN: 978-1-5127-0599-7 (hc)
ISBN: 978-1-5127-0597-3 (e)

Library of Congress Control Number: 2015912279

Print information available on the last page.

WestBow Press rev. date: 8/28/2015

CONTENTS

Dedication vii
Foreword ix
Introduction: A Conquered Conqueror: "What Now, Lord?" xi

1. Born for Trouble 1
2. The School of Uncertainty 12
3. My "Baby" and Our Baby 28
4. Decision of Destruction 37
5. Welcome to the DOC (Department of Corrections) 44
6. Doing the Unthinkable 54
7. History Repeats Itself 60
8. Indiana Intervention 71
9. Born of the Spirit 78
10. Living the Gospel 85
11. Testing Time 94
12. The Call of God 109
13. New Life, New Wife 117
14. Captain Conqueror 125
15. Transforming the World 135

Epilogue: A Life-Changing Moment 151
About the Author 153

DEDICATION

I would like to dedicate this book to my life partner, best friend, and wife, Stefanie Benson. Without her, I would not be where I am in my life and walk with the Lord!

FOREWORD

More than a Conqueror is a special book that will be an encouragement to anyone who reads it. It was difficult to put down. It will be a timely and special blessing, especially for those whose lives have not begun the way they would have hoped or planned. It isn't how we begin that matters; it is how we finish.

This book describes and shows God's redemption for a person who came to the end of himself, looked up and cried out to the Lord. As always, God met him exactly where he was and took him on a journey of faith—the journey of a lifetime.

We didn't know Mike in his early days. However, the Mike we know and love is "fired up" about Jesus. He lives his faith daily and continues to seek God as he shares his story and life vulnerably with all who will listen. Mike is anointed to take the message of Jesus Christ to his generation effectively.

This is a book that will give hope to those who may feel hopeless. *More than a Conqueror* shows the overcoming power of God when infused into the spirit of a man hungry for more of Him. It is a book that will encourage anyone who has overcome or who is in the process of overcoming.

Thanks, Mike, for writing your story and for bringing all glory to God in the process. Second Corinthians 3:2–3 (NLT) says,

> The only letter of recommendation we need is you yourselves. Your lives are a letter written in our

> hearts; everyone can read it and recognize our good work among you. Clearly, you are a letter from Christ showing the result of our ministry among you. This "letter" is written not with pen and ink, but with the Spirit of the living God. It is carved not on tablets of stone, but on human hearts.

There is nobody like our God, and there is nothing impossible with Him.

Wally and June Blume
Owners, Denali Flavors, makers of Moose Tracks Ice Cream

INTRODUCTION

A Conquered Conqueror: "What Now, Lord?"

I began writing this book in September of a very dark year for me, 2013. It was the eighth year I was in ministry, and to call that year challenging would be a crazy understatement. In January 2013, I suffered a stroke, of all things. I was sitting on the couch with my wife, Stefanie, and I was feeling very fatigued. She commented that I looked tired and suggested that I go downstairs and go to bed.

As I was walking toward the stairs, I suddenly lost all feeling in my right side. My right arm went numb and nothing would work, so I went crashing to the floor. I tried as hard as I could to get up, but I couldn't move my right side at all. I was stuck right there on the floor.

"Mike, what's going on?" Stefanie was up in a flash and leaning over me, asking me questions. "What's wrong?"

"I'm okay. I just got a little dizzy," I told her—or so I *thought* I told her. It sounded clear enough to me, but from the look on her face, I knew something wasn't right. We weren't communicating.

What Stefanie heard coming out of my mouth was a bunch of garbled mumbo jumbo. She kept asking me questions, and I kept thinking I was answering, but I could see that her distress was increasing every time I opened my mouth.

She grabbed the phone and stood over me while she dialed 911. As concerned as she was, she was so used to my pranks that she still took the time to threaten me: "Mike, you better not be joking with me!" she kept saying. "I'm calling an ambulance, so you better *stop it* if you're joking!"

I admit, I had that coming. I have been known to pull a prank or two on her, but this was definitely not a prank.

Stefanie quickly reached the 911 operator, who directed her to ask me some questions. That didn't help my wife's mindset any since each time I answered her, it was in more of the same garbled speech. I could see the panic building on her face, so I just stopped talking.

Our kids, Sofia and Ryland, were sleeping in the bedroom right at the top of the stairs. I thank the Lord that they were asleep at the time, so they didn't hear any of what was going on. They didn't have to see their father lying helpless on the ground like that, mumbling words that made no sense.

As I was lying there motionless, I couldn't help but wonder, *What's happening to me?* At the same time, though, I felt a sense of peace. I had peace in my spirit, and I knew everything was going to be all right because God had a plan for my life. Ever since I was a little kid, He'd had a plan. Even before I was born, He'd had a plan! That much I was sure of, even lying there on the floor. I was born for a purpose; I was on this planet for a reason. So are you and every other person God has created. We just have to discover and follow His plan. I knew His plan for me was still in process, so I had a peace that He would get us through whatever was going on with me.

Soon an ambulance showed up, along with several fire department volunteers and the police. Suddenly, my living room was full of people—six paramedics in all had shown up. Emergency personnel were trying to get me up on the stretcher, which, seeing as I weighed in at close to 300 pounds, was a feat of strength equal to anything the Conquerors strength team pulls off! Finally, they managed to lift me onto the gurney, carry me down my steps, and put me in the ambulance.

My in-laws stayed back with the kids, and my wife climbed into the front seat of the ambulance with one paramedic. I was lying there in the back, of course, still thinking about my life, while the other paramedic kept an eye on me. My life didn't flash before me, the way some people experience in a medical crisis. But I laid there wondering, *What next, Lord?*

As the sound of the siren echoed through the streets of Jenison, Michigan, I also wondered at one point, *Will I make it out of this one?* My life has been filled with difficulties and challenges, hardship and turmoil all along, but I have never felt as helpless as I did at that moment. *Will my life ever be the same?* I asked myself. *Whatever's happening, it's bad and it's major!* I had to wonder if this was the end of life as I knew it. I've been through a lot of personal tests over the years, and I saw this as another test, or maybe an attack of the enemy. Was I now a conquered conqueror? Or was it an opportunity to be more than a conqueror? I remember praying, *My life and my times are not in my hands; they're in Yours, Lord. Let me know what to do next . . .*

As the ambulance rushed me toward the hospital, the paramedic put me on some IVs. Once he got those in, he started asking me questions. About halfway to the hospital, I started to talk to him, and he yelled up to Stefanie and the driver that I was talking, even though I wasn't making any sense. When he asked me what year it was, I told him 2016!

By the time we pulled into the hospital's emergency entrance, I had started to recover some of the feeling in my right side. I even sat up as the paramedics were taking me out of the ambulance. They kept asking me questions again, like "What day is it?"

"Anthrax" was my answer to that one. I laugh at it now, but at the time, it didn't seem very funny to my wife or family!

My sister Alicia works as a nurse at the hospital where I was taken. She came down to the ER, and so did my mom and my niece Kaeliegh. It struck me as kind of funny that everyone else was freaking out at first, even though I was the one in the hospital bed.

My good friend Pastor Bernie Blaukamp also came down from my home church, Resurrection Life Church in Grandville, Michigan. I love him as a father figure, and he has mentored me for almost ten years. Having him with me really helped. He stood at the foot of my bed and prayed, bringing all the support of my church family with him. That brought me so much peace.

I spent five days in the hospital while the doctors tried to find a reason behind the stroke. One time, four neuroscientists were standing in my hospital room, all scratching their heads because they couldn't believe what they were seeing. They kept running more tests, trying to find out what caused the stroke. One said I'd need speech therapy to talk again, but in the end I didn't even need it.

My brain scans clearly showed two areas of damage. The spot with the most damage was in the area of my speech center. The secondary damage, which was not as bad but was still pretty significant, was in the area of my brain that controlled physical strength. Looking at it from an outside perspective, some would say that's kind of an ironic diagnosis for a member of the Conquerors strength team, which travels all over doing feats of strength and preaching the Gospel, and they would be right.

I knew that a coordinated attack of the enemy, the devil, was behind the stroke. And the stroke didn't just come out of the blue, because I realize now that I had opened doors for him. I had opened doors through compromise and through some supplements I was taking. I had also opened doors through abusing Adderall. Adderall is a drug they give mostly to young people with ADHD, but it was prescribed for me over quite a few years because of my sleep apnea. I had sleep apnea that bordered on narcolepsy. Driving down the road I could fall asleep behind the wheel, even if I had gotten plenty of sleep the night before—eight or ten hours.

Initially, doctors put me on a CPAP machine, so I slept well and got plenty of rest. But I would still fall asleep at odd (or dangerous) moments, so they put me on Adderall in addition to the machine. People who know me will tell you that my personality is very amped up as it is. Adderall just added to that. One of its side effects is excitability—not something I needed any more of! I felt as if I were ten feet tall and bulletproof on that stuff! My years of taking Adderall, both the prescribed amount and sometimes *more* than the prescribed amount, had taken a toll on my system.

I had also gotten complacent. I had reached a point where I felt as though I were on "coast," and I was no longer believing God about where the money for our ministry support would come from. We had a very good partner base, so the financial support was going well and the Conquerors' ministry had grown. My influence had spread along with that, and I became comfortable—very comfortable. In all those ways, I had set myself up for a big fall. And it happened in the form of a stroke.

After the stroke, I remember praying and seeking the Lord. In response, He showed me a vision of myself. I was sitting in a chair, and He walked up beside me and put His arm around me. Then He patted my shoulder and said, "Good job, Son! Good job! Now, follow Me." Then He began to walk away in a line that angled off into the distance.

I watched myself in the vision, sitting there in the chair. I noticed that I reached both my hands down and grabbed tightly to the sides of the chair, and then I hung on with all my might. That is where I believe I opened the door for the enemy, through my compromise and through my laziness. It reminds me of the story of King David when he was "resting." The Bible says that he was resting at the time when kings go to war. (You can read more of the story in 2 Samuel chapter 11.) David used to fight for the kingdom back when Saul was king. Then he spent years being chased by Saul and hiding in caves. After he became the king himself, he spent more years fighting battles and building his kingdom. Finally, he reached this place of complacency where a battle came along and he said to himself, *I'll just sit this one out.*

It was sad that it was time for David to go to war, but he would not go. He sent others in his place instead, and he certainly found his share of trouble on the homefront as a result! That was the time when he got into trouble by seeing Bathsheba from up on his roof and committing adultery with her. He got her pregnant and killed her husband to hide it. Her husband who was away—you guessed it—fighting the battle that David should have been out there fighting, too. As the Scriptures show, things spiraled downhill for David pretty fast after that. He had some serious repenting to do.

That's what I feel happened to me. I got weary and complacent, and I started to work harder and harder, but my priorities were out of order. That left the door wide open for the enemy to come in and try to take me out. But God is a miracle God. God is a redeeming God. God is a God of hope and a God of love and a God of the future. He still had His hand on my life in spite of my failings. I only ended up spending five days in the hospital, which was amazing. I was so grateful, but even after I was released, I hadn't reached the end of my dark times. I started dealing with post-stroke depression, or PSD. It is considered one of the most frequent neuropsychiatric consequences of having a stroke. (That even sounds scary, doesn't it?) Basically, it's a mood disorder that can involve major episodes of depression and even manic episodes. (Think about my personality combined with a manic episode. That sounds even more scary!)

I had never faced anything like PSD before. I just didn't feel right no matter what I did, and the whole thing put some, well, downright depressing limits on my ministry. The stroke limited my ability to think straight (temporarily), so I was not making sound decisions. The stroke also weakened me physically, so I was on hiatus from doing feats of strength with the Conquerors team. I basically felt as if I had lost control of everything.

Desperate to feel any way other than the way I was feeling, I started down the road of one of my former bad habits. I didn't let it affect me to the point where it was obvious to those around me, but I was using it as a comfort measure, to make me feel better—or at least to feel different. I hid my intense struggle with PSD and my return to my old habit from my wife, as well as from my pastor.

From that point, I saw myself slowly spiraling downhill, and I knew things would soon get even more out of control. I also knew I was taking unacceptable risks with all that had been entrusted to me—my family, my ministry, and the life and health God had given back to me after my hospitalization. Yet I just couldn't seem to put the brakes on and climb back up to where I needed to be. As I said, I wasn't feeling like myself or acting like myself, and I wasn't making the choices I would normally have made back before the stroke sideswiped me.

I don't say that by way of excuse—I had no excuse for my poor choices. But that time in my life showed me more than ever that our righteousness is not in ourselves; it comes from God through Christ's finished work of taking our sins upon Himself on the cross. (Good thing for me!) It was only through God's grace and mercy that things turned around for me.

My wife was so gracious during this time. She literally extended the grace of God to me, knowing that I wasn't myself. She stood by me and intervened on my behalf. I made her a little crazy during that time (actually, more than a little), and we did reach one point where we were almost ready to split apart and call it quits on our marriage. But I am so thankful that neither God nor Stefanie would let the enemy have me; they stood strong with me when I wasn't doing a great job of standing strong myself. I will never forget what they did for me, or the unconditional love they showed me. I am a better man and a better minister because of it.

Back in that hospital bed, when I had asked again, "What now, Lord?" He had given me an exciting answer. It took me awhile to walk in it, but once I understood how the PSD affected me physically and how my compromise and complacency affected me spiritually, I was able to get back on my feet, with God's help and Stefanie's. I was back on track with God's plan for my life once again.

Specifically, the exciting answer the Lord had given me was, "Your time of trials and testing is over. Your time of fruitfulness has begun." This book you hold in your hands is a kind of firstfruits of that promise. I dedicate these pages to Him and offer them to you, praying that my story will bring you hope and introduce you to the One who bought me hope when I was hopeless and alone, locked in a lonely prison cell for what should have been years and years to come. Because of Him, here I stand, set free both physically and spiritually.

My goal in writing this book for you, and our goal as the Conquerors strength team, is to reach as many people as possible all over the world with the good news that they, too, can be set free. They can overcome their past and be conquerors in their future, fulfilling all of the good plan that God the Father has for them. I pray that *More than a Conqueror* will bring hope to millions of people who want to live the life of a conqueror through Jesus Christ. I pray that it will bring hope and life to *you*. Always remember that you have available to you all the power and love of the real Strongman, Jesus Christ.

1

Born for Trouble

Jack and Rosemarie Benson lived on the southwest side of Detroit, Michigan. They had met while working at a small factory that made boxes. They fell in love there, and they got married shortly afterward. Both had faced extreme hardship while growing up and had somehow overcome it and managed to survive.

Jack had contracted polio as a child, and the disease left him with a handicap that affected his entire right side. At least he had a comfortable childhood home, though. He lived with his mother and his stepfather, who worked at what was then the local Fisher Body plant. His stepfather was able to provide a nice lifestyle for the family in Dearborn.

Rosemarie's childhood had not been so comfortable. She grew up in Detroit in abject poverty and in a low-income area that was riddled with crime. Her father was an angry and abusive man, both physically and verbally.

Now, in spite of their early difficulties, Jack and Rosemarie had each other. They were determined to love each other the best way they knew how and to give any children who came along better lives than the ones they had known growing up. It wasn't long before they got the chance to try. On November 14, 1972, I became their firstborn. Two years later, I was followed by my sister Alicia. The two of us were inseparable. We definitely felt love in our household when we were tiny, and we loved each other (and still do). I would follow Alicia around when she first began to walk, holding my hands under her in case she fell down.

My mom worked hard during the day and went to school at night. She was studying to be a tool and die maker. She had landed a job as a custodian at General Motors (formerly Fisher Body), and she decided to work at becoming a tool and die maker so she could provide a better future for her kids. Alicia and I—and, later on, our younger sister, Christine—were our mom's whole world.

My dad's handicap prevented him from getting a good job anywhere, so he mostly stayed home and took care of us. He became a stay-at-home dad long before it was in style the way it is now, which made my mom feel resentful. But it was what they had to do to make ends meet and take care of us, so they did it. Even though they had come out of such tumultuous backgrounds and still faced challenges every day, they tried their best to provide a better environment for my sisters and me. To this day I am grateful to them, even though I did not always make the best use of the advantages they tried to give me.

Off to School

When I was three or four years old, my family was able to move out of the city of Detroit and into a suburb of Dearborn like the one my dad had grown up in. My parents saw it as a step up, and it was a good move for us. That's where I began school. I thought school was fun, and I really enjoyed going—up until second grade. Then things began to go in a negative direction for me.

My family was Catholic at the time, so we were raised in the Catholic Church and attended the Catholic school. In my second grade, we had two aquariums in class—one containing fish and the other tadpoles. In my second-grade mind, I wondered why the fish always seemed so interested in the tadpoles. They kept looking at them through the glass, almost like they wanted to play. One day, I decided I would unite the tadpoles with the fish so that they could meet each other and swim together. *What a great idea!* I thought.

When I got a chance, I quietly walked over to the tanks and put a couple of tadpoles into the fish tank. To my horror, the fish *ate* the tadpoles! I hurried back to my seat so no one would know what I had done. There was a small problem, though—a female problem whose name was Sally. She had witnessed my attempts at aquatic matchmaking and had seen the fish having lunch, compliments of me. As soon as everyone was seated, she raised her hand and proceeded to tell the nun (our teacher) what I had done.

The nun took me by the ear and brought me to the front of the class. She then proceeded to bend me over her knee and spank me with a ruler, the whole time telling everyone what a bad boy I was. Those words hurt more than the sting I felt on my backside. The humiliation and the suddenness of my punishment cut deep. I'd had no chance to explain what I was really trying to do; I wasn't trying to be mean or malicious. Yet the nun's words, "You're such a bad, bad boy," kept ringing in my ears the whole time I was being punished and for a long time afterward.

I was not a bad boy at the time of the tadpole fiasco, but I was about to become one very bad, bad boy. I now realize that this was a pivotal moment in my young life, and one that would mark me for a long time. The words of the nun compounded the words my dad had begun to feed me at home.

"Big dummy!" my dad would call me. Or he would say, "You're never going to amount to anything!"

I know I am not the only child who has ever heard those kinds of negative, destructive words. If you heard them too, you know how damaging they can be. Now I was getting them both at home and at school—a double blow. Those words caused a hatred to rise up within me—a hatred for church, God, parental authority, and anyone or anything that represented authority over me.

From that time on, I did everything I could to avoid school. I would fake sickness and cry to my mom about how I wanted to stay home because I didn't feel well. I remember one time when I was dropped off at school, I attempted to open the doors but couldn't, so I figured, *Hey, there must not be school today.*

A few seconds later, a nun opened the door and said, "Come on in, young man."

Instead, I ran home as fast as I could. Our house was only a few blocks down the street, and I made a beeline for it! Once I got there, I told my mom I didn't feel well and begged her to let me stay home. She relented, and I got to spend the rest of that day at home.

Sometimes I would walk to school. This was back in the day when a kid could walk to school safely, even in the neighborhood I lived in. Our house was directly across the street from Herman Gardens, a notorious housing project known for drugs and violent crime. On my way to school, I had to pass an old, abandoned house on one of the corners, which happened to be a hangout for some kids from the project. Each time I would walk by, they would call me names, try to steal my lunch box, and generally push me around.

I got no sympathy at home and no help dealing with the situation. My dad was not much help since he had grown up in a sheltered environment and didn't have the street sense to deal with the realities of life on the streets of Detroit. My mom, who had grown up on those streets, did not want me to grow up without learning how to defend myself. She figured if I took a few hard knocks in the process, then that was just part of life. Same thing with my uncles, my mother's brothers. They were notorious for the fights they got into. It seemed as if violence ran in our family. One day one of my uncles came to our house and sat down to have a talk with me.

"Whenever there's a group of kids after you and you're outnumbered," my uncle said to me, "you gotta find an equalizer."

"What's an equalizer?" I asked.

He said, "Something that will even the odds, like a stick or a pipe. Just pick something up and hit one of 'em as hard as you can right on the noggin! And then watch 'em all run!"

The next day, an opportunity to try out the advice my uncle had given me presented itself. It was the usual scenario playing out, but this time the kids pushed me into the abandoned house and had me cornered.

One of them started taunting me. "What you gonna do now, boy? Huh? What you gonna do?"

I felt a boiling anger rise up within me, and I remembered what my uncle had said. I reached down and picked up a board, but I didn't notice the nail sticking out of the end of it. I was only focused on one thing—the head of the nearest bully. I hit him as hard as I could right in the head, and blood came gushing out all over the place.

The other boys ran out of the abandoned house, along with their injured friend. I stood there inside, all by myself, still holding that board, and a funny feeling came over me. The anger boiling on the inside of me felt *good*, especially when I vented it on that kid. I didn't really realize it at the time, but it brought a release of the pain and frustration I had been feeling in my heart. In the moment, I just realized that I really liked the way it made me feel. Right then, I made an inner vow: *I will never let anyone hurt me ever again!*

Needless to say, I did not see those boys up close after that incident. I walked to school with my head held high, and that felt good too. Really good.

On the Move

When I was about to enter fifth grade, my family made a move out of the Detroit area. Mom had gotten laid off from her job at General Motors, and she decided we should move out in the country to be near her sister Clara and brother-in-law Gary. It was a big change for my sister Alicia and me, leaving everything we had known behind for a new, fresh start. In fact, from that point on we moved around quite a bit. With each move came a new school district where we had to make new friends. I began feeling as if I was always the new kid, which came with both its benefits and drawbacks. It was exciting to make new friends, and not so exciting to make new enemies.

Our move away from Detroit took us to a little house on the outskirts of Port Sanilac, a fishing town right on Lake Huron. Alicia and I adjusted quickly to the new "country" environment. We were excited to have so much open space to run and play in. But the hurt and hunger in my heart could not be soothed or healed by simply changing locations. My parents thought changing locations would mean a better outcome for us, and in some ways it did. They thought getting us away from the street life that Mom grew up in would somehow insulate us from the kind of pain and hardship she had suffered in her childhood. But we had our own kind of pain going on. At least, I did. I was already becoming scarred on the inside. Mom successfully removed us from her former environment, but the move did not change the environment developing in our hearts.

Changing a person's geographical location is not an effective way to change a person's life, because we live our lives from the inside out. You may be able to change your outward circumstances; you may be able to change your location. But those changes are unlikely to produce the type of change needed to change the direction of your life.

So trouble did not follow me from one location to the next; it was inside me! It was the result of the void left in my heart from having a dad who wasn't able to offer me what I needed from him to fill that void inside. And it resulted from having a mom who was doing her best to give us a better life outwardly, but who didn't have a clue about how to live life inwardly or teach us how to do that. Living through such a miserable childhood, Mom had never had a stable, loving home environment modeled for her. But I know she really was doing the best she could, with no prior knowledge about how to give us kids what we needed deep down on the inside.

Alicia and I were accepted into the small community school of Carson City, just a few miles from Port Sanilac. By this time I had learned the power behind the fists, and I wielded them well. It wasn't long before I was in my first fight. Somehow it seemed as if I was a bully magnet. Sure enough, one day out on the playground, the school bully made his move. I'll call him Billy. We were playing a game of "football" we called "smear the queer"—not very politically correct, I know, but that was our name for it. Billy tackled me from behind, and I didn't even have the ball!

I got up and proceeded to beat Billy up, ensuring a place for myself in the elementary school pecking order, and also ensuring myself a trip to the principal's office. The school gave me a break, though, being a new kid and all. They called my parents, but they didn't suspend me. Of course, my parents defended me and bailed me out of the trouble I had gotten myself into.

Getting into "Real" Trouble

You can take people out of the streets, but you can't take the streets out of people. I seemed to be living proof of that. This was the time in my life when I got into my first "official" trouble, and my cousin played a part in it. We were at the local Big Wheel store and decided to "five-finger discount" some things we wanted. We were getting away with it, and in our excitement, our huge young egos prompted us to take some caps (those little exploding ones that came in a roll) off the shelf in the toy aisle and beat them with a nearby baseball bat. That quickly got the attention of store security! Before we knew it, we were in the office behind the "secret" glass, the glass stores have where they can watch you but you can't see them. We were scared and busted.

Dad and one of my uncles came to the store to get us. I figured I could talk my way out of this one, so we came home smiling. But it seemed like the whole family was gathered together, waiting to deal with us. My mom gave me the spanking of a lifetime, but my corporal punishment was nothing compared to what my cousin got. It sounded like World War II in the room next door; I heard nothing but him yelling as he got a beatdown.

But after my cousin got whipped, that was it. For him it was over, and he was free to carry on with his normal routine. On the other hand, in addition to the worst spanking ever, I got the worst thing imaginable on top of it. I got grounded for a month! At that time a month seemed like an eternity to me, and I hated the fact that I would be consigned to home while Alicia was out playing.

My troubles didn't end there, though. On Christmas I received every boy's dream gift, a BB gun. I soon found that shooting birds, squirrels, snakes and other assorted woodland creatures, or tin cans, was not enough of a thrill, so I resorted to shooting my neighbors' windows. It wasn't hard for the neighbors to figure out who the culprit was, seeing as we were the only neighbors. One neighbor had seen me time and time again outside shooting everything that could move, so he knew just where to lay the blame for his shattered windows. Once again, I was in trouble. It seemed as if from the day I was born, I was created to get into trouble!

I was also involved in one other window-breaking incident. I don't know what this fascination I had with windows was. I just felt this pressure to break them. I went into town one day and went to the house of this kid who was not very popular at school. I proceeded to break his windows. Not all of them, just a couple. When his parents came to my house looking for the culprit, I thought I would be grounded, but that all changed when they verbally attacked my parents and me. My mother and father were so offended that they forgot about what I had done, and I didn't even get in any trouble for it. At the end of that encounter, they were thinking, *This kid deserved to have his windows broken*. I was in full agreement!

These incidents were the start of a childhood full of trouble. After that, it seemed I was always fighting and always breaking things.

Becoming a Court Case

Eventually General Motors put my mom back to work at a plant in Grand Rapids, so once again our family was on the move. We went to a new city, a new neighborhood, a new school district, a new everything. It was hard moving all over again, but we did get to spend the summer at a lake just south of Grand Rapids called Green Lake. That was probably one of the best summers of my entire childhood. I spent the summer swimming and playing with Alicia and the neighborhood kids, and not once did I get into trouble.

We finally settled in a duplex in Kentwood, a suburb of Grand Rapids. I was in fifth grade, again, and I was the new kid, again. That meant I had to establish myself all over again. Due to being from Detroit, I quickly got a reputation as the "city kid," which I didn't mind at all. I had developed the mindset that I had to protect myself, so I came in thinking I had to become the toughest, baddest kid of them all, and do it fast. I didn't waste any time accomplishing my goal!

Those Kentwood years were a time of firsts for me, and not in a good way. One of the "firsts" was my first time smoking a cigarette. Some neighborhood kids introduced me to smoking. We lived at the end of a cul-de-sac that was situated right next to the entrance to a local park. The park was full of trails, and I used to cut through it walking to school. Some of the older kids liked to hang out under the pavilion located in the center of the park. One day as I was walking by, some kids were there on their bikes. They were smoking cigarettes, and they yelled for me to come on over. Curious about what they wanted, I went over.

"Hey, do you smoke?" one of the kids asked me.

"Yeah," I answered, not wanting to feel like an outsider.

One kid handed me a lit cigarette, which I proceeded to puff on, just the way I saw it done in the movies.

"Let me see you inhale!" another kid said.

It was obvious that I didn't know what that meant, so one of the other kids began to show me how to inhale. I took my first real drag off a cigarette, and it made me cough uncontrollably and feel sick to my stomach. Then I became dizzy, and everything started spinning.

The kids all stood around laughing at me, which made me angry. So I took another drag, and another, and another, determined that I was not going to let them laugh at me. I showed them I was tough and could handle anything they threw my way. Of course, they didn't see me heaving my guts out once I got down one of the trials and out of their sight.

I also had another encounter with the law while we lived in Kentwood. Next door to us was another duplex. The family living there included a son my age and an older sister. We got along pretty well, and we played together in their sandbox. I don't remember exactly what happened, but somehow my sister and I got into a feud with these kids. I decided I would once again get my trusty BB gun out and dole out some justice. From our basement, I had a clear shot at the older sister's bedroom window. I proceeded to place two BBs right through it.

I figured it was the perfect crime. I mean, who would ever know it was me who fired those shots out of our basement? It could have been anyone, or some random act of vandalism, right? I was sure they would *never* figure out the trajectory of the BBs and would *never* notice the two exit holes through the screen that I shot through.

A little while after I pulled the trigger, I heard a knock on our door. Mom opened the door to find a Kentwood police officer standing there.

"Ma'am," he said, "your son may have been involved with some damage to your neighbors' property."

Mom immediately called me upstairs and asked if I knew anything about it.

"No, Mom, I don't know anything!" I told her in front of the police officer. Lying was a tactic I used to cover up things and distract and deceive people. I became highly proficient at it during my childhood.

The police officer asked if he could look downstairs, and my mom gave him permission. In the basement, he went straight to the window I had shot the BBs out of and looked at the screen.

"Explain these holes in the screen here," he told me.

"I was poking a pencil through that screen," I lied again.

He then proceeded to take a pencil out of his pocket, and he attempted to push it through the holes that were already there. Alarmingly, the pencil was way too large to fit through the holes. Confronted with the evidence, I finally confessed.

The police officer handed my parents a summons to appear before a judge, and then he left. I was in deep trouble, to say the least! Once again I was grounded, and we almost had Christmas taken away from us on top of it.

A couple weeks later, I stood alongside my parents before a judge. The judge ordered my parents to pay restitution to our neighbors, and he ordered me to go next door personally and apologize to them. He also gave me a strong warning about the path I was going down. I didn't heed his warning, but I wish I would have. I had officially become a court case for the first time, but it wouldn't be the last time. Not by a long shot.

2

The School of Uncertainty

In school I was always the cool kid. I grew my hair long in back, wore heavy metal T-shirts, and even had one of those Michael Jackson jackets with all the zippers everywhere. I always had this deep insecurity in my heart, so I always felt as if I needed to project a tough image to protect myself. I never had anyone model for me what it was to be a man, so I faced my growing-up years with a lot of uncertainty. I wanted to become a man, but I didn't know how.

I could have used some guidance and advice as I grew into young manhood, the kind only a father can give, but I did not get any from my dad because he simply didn't know how to give it. He just didn't have the skills and abilities to sow into me what I needed, so I grabbed on to the substitutes for manhood the culture around me was offering. I got my idea of "being a man" from MTV, heavy metal music, and movies on TV.

My dad was born in the 1940s. When my grandfather found out that my dad had contracted polio as a child, a disease that affected his entire right side, my grandfather just couldn't face it. He left my grandmother and their diseased son, so my dad never really knew his father and never received the love and comfort that would have produced security in a young boy. Instead, he was rejected by his dad, and he carried all the scars of that into his own attempts at fatherhood.

Probably because of the polio, my dad grew up living a sheltered life. He was always under my grandmother's protection, and she never prepared him for the real world. She never taught him that life was rough or that he would have to face some serious challenges as someone who was "different." Grandma insulated her disabled son for as long as she could, but in the long run, I think it did him more harm than good. I think that even as an adult, my dad was insecure. He wasn't a man of many words, and he only took action when my mom told him to. It was as if he was incapable of handling anything himself and had just given up trying. I know his attitudes and behaviors had an effect on us kids. As I said, Dad just didn't seem to have what it took to give us what we needed from him.

On the bright side, Grandma eventually remarried, and this time her new husband worked hard for his family and did his best to care for my dad. All my life, I knew my dad's stepfather as "Poppy," and Poppy really was a great man! But men of Poppy's generation were not much on expressing their feelings or learning how to deal with them effectively. Poppy did the best he could to handle the situation he married into, but that didn't heal the wounds of the past. The deep hurts my father carried inside his heart as a young boy remained. When I came along as the next generation and was wounded in turn by my dad, I was just the continuation of a long line of broken, wounded hearts.

Growing up, I did whatever I could on my own to figure out who I was as a man, what this thing called life was all about, and what my purpose in life was. But without any strong male role models to guide me, my efforts left me frustrated and angry. I didn't know it at the time, but the bad behavior that resulted was my way of lashing out at those who were in authority. My "bad boy" image and behavior were also a way of venting my frustration. I embraced my identity as a tough guy because I thought that's what manhood was all about. All my heroes on TV were the bad guys. I loved Mafia movies and any other movies where the bad guys were glorified, and I wanted to be as tough as they were.

Girls, Girls, Girls!

Eventually we moved to the other side of Grand Rapids, to the suburb of Grandville. We rented a house on Ivanrest Avenue when I was going into sixth grade. Somehow I made it through all the adjustments of a new neighborhood and new school *again,* and I started middle school in seventh grade at Grandville Public Schools. I remember that it seemed like a big deal to all of us elementary students to be assigned our own lockers and go to different classes with different teachers.

Of course, the best part about middle school was the girls! Up until that time, I had not been interested in the opposite sex. I had been more interested in guns, football, and hanging out with my friends. But all that changed in middle school. There were girls, girls, girls everywhere, and it was as if I were really seeing them for the first time!

Since I didn't have a strong model of manhood at home to learn from, I had to learn about it for myself. I did not choose the greatest place to learn about anything, let alone learn how to become a man. I immersed myself in the rock-and-roll culture, at least the wannabe culture. Part of that culture was drugs, and another part was sex. I discovered both of those at an early age—too early. I won't share my exploits with you in detail, but I had many sexual experiences with women who were sometimes decades older than I was. I thought at the time that I was being a "real" man—you were a man if you had sex with as many women as possible, right? I thought so. Little did I know that I was setting myself up to distort my manhood in a way that would take years of healing to overcome. It would be a long time before my sense of manhood was restored to its original, healthy intent.

Middle school was also the first time I experienced drinking. The local roller rink was the place for us to hang out in middle school. Every Friday we would gather there and skate in circles, wearing the tightest jeans possible. Everyone was there just to be cool and to see who was skating with whom and who might get into a fight.

One night a friend and I got together with a high school student who found a buyer for us. We bought a fifth of Strawberry Schnapps and proceeded to guzzle it down. I remember the feeling I got that first time being drunk. I was laughing so hard, stumbling around, and feeling numb. I know we were walking around outside the rink without skates on, and I remember bits and pieces of that night, but not much else. But boy oh boy, I remember the next morning! You would think that vomiting up anything you put in your stomach and feeling like a semitruck ran over your head would deter anyone from drinking again. But not me. For me, it was the status symbol of using alcohol that attracted me, way more than the buzz I got from being drunk. Now I had become one of the "cool" kids because I could talk about my drunken exploits from the night before.

I started acting just like my rock-and-roll idols, which at the time were the Motley Crue. Those were my heroes, with their long hair, drugs, booze, and women! I wanted to be just like them, and I did everything I could to emulate them. When there is lack of identity, lack of character and lack of a solid foundation built into young people by their parents, they will turn to all the wrong role models. I was looking for a place to fit in, to belong, a place where I would be accepted for who I was. The problem was that I did not have a clue who I was, what I was created to be or the purpose I was created for. And on top of all that, I felt deep pain in my heart, which fostered deep-seated frustration and anger in me.

The Next Level of Lawlessness

After about a year of living in a rented house on Ivanrest, my parents purchased a double-wide mobile home and we moved into a nearby mobile home park. I quickly befriended a neighbor who was a couple grades ahead of me, and we formed a ragtag gang of teens who walked everywhere together, carrying my ghetto blaster and blaring out loud music that I'm sure everyone in the neighborhood appreciated. (Or not!) We often hung out at the Laundromat across from the trailer park and played video games, smoked cigarettes, or picked fights when the opportunity came up.

One night a friend and I were out walking the neighborhood with a girl we knew, and we stopped at a house where her brother was hanging out. Inside, four guys were sitting around in the living room. They all had long hair and looked quite a bit older. One of them was rolling what looked like a cigarette. The girl we were with asked us, "Have you ever smoked weed before?"

I actually had not, but I wanted to be cool, so I said "Oh yeah." When the joint came to me, I took a big drag on it. I had been watching everyone who had the joint before me and I noticed they held the drag in for a long time, so I did the same. I didn't feel anything at first, no instant rush or tingling sensation anywhere. But by the time the joint had been passed around four times, I was feeling *real* good. We walked out into the crisp air of the early winter night, and I was as high as a kite. Thus my love for marijuana began. We all decided to go to our favorite pizza place after we got high. Once we got inside, back into the warm air, the uncontrollable laughter started. We laughed our heads off for no apparent reason, and man, we put a hurting on those pizzas!

I quickly went from substance experimentation to substance abuse. What started out as fun slowly became a problem, one that I would face a long battle with, and one that would cause much hurt and damage in my life. The very thing I was looking to for comforting all the pain in my heart was adding more hurt and pain. We often look to things that will make us feel better, especially when we don't know how to deal with the root causes of the pain inside us.

With my substance abuse came crime. I started stealing from my parents and from anyone else I could. My friends and I needed the money so we could go to our buyer and purchase alcohol, or every once in a while buy some marijuana. With no moral compass and no role model to exemplify how a young man ought to carry himself, I had no regard for people, their property, or the law. With these new developments into drugs and stealing, this was about the time that my bad behavior really started getting the attention of law enforcement people.

One of my friends who was a little bit older than me lived on a street nearby. He had a stepdad he didn't like, and he often complained about the man. One day this friend told me they would be leaving for a few days, and he would see me when he came back. One of my cousins and I decided we were going to break into their trailer while they were gone.

We did break in and began by eating some food out of the fridge. Then we proceeded to raid the liquor cabinet. Once we were well intoxicated, we got the urge to destroy things, so we did. We threw all the contents of the fridge out onto the counters, the living room carpet, and everywhere else we could. We smashed glass and anything else we could get our hands on. Then we decided to slit the parents' water bed with a knife. As water poured out all over the place, flooding half the trailer, we decided it was time to get out of there!

We justified our actions of vandalizing the trailer by telling ourselves that we were getting back at my friend's stepdad back for him. And we didn't touch my friend's room or his sister's room, which provided the clue that would later lead to our arrest. I also pretty much had no conscience at that point. I was completely lost, heading down a road that later would almost cost me my life. I didn't realize it, of course, but my actions were partly a reaction to the anger that I felt deep down inside and partly a cry for help.

When that family returned home, they were in utter shock at the disaster that awaited them. I remember when my friend came to my door and told me the news about the vandalism done in his trailer. He asked me if I had heard anything or if I knew anything.

Of course, I lied through my teeth—something I was already quite adept at doing. All I could do was think about the trouble I would be in if they found out the truth, so I was willing to deny any involvement to the bitter end. Then a couple days later, my parents and I were asked to come down to the City of Wyoming Police Department (the trailer park was in the suburb of Wyoming). Somehow I knew I was busted; I just couldn't figure out how.

I knew nothing of forensics except what I had watched on TV, and I had been figuring there was no way anyone could find out it was me who vandalized the trailer. I mean, after all, the kid who lived there and I were friends. No one would suspect me of having any involvement. But forensic evidence does not lie, as I was doing. The detective I saw asked me for my shoes, which would explain why my mom had brought an extra pair for me to put on. Then the detective proceeded to question me about my whereabouts on the night in question. I had snuck out on the night in question, along with my cousin, so my mom confirmed what I told the police, that I was sound asleep in my room. She didn't know any differently. We were then free to leave the station. The detective told me I would get my shoes back when they were done with them.

I thought I had gotten away with my act of vandalism, and that I had outsmarted the police! That is, until we got a call from the same detective the next day, again requesting our presence at the police station. This time they spoke to me alone, with my mom's permission. She figured since her son was innocent, what could be the harm in it?

The detective sat across a plain table in a plain room and started out with an assertion rather than a question: "Mike, we know you vandalized your neighbors' trailer."

"No, no, not me," I said.

The detective pressed on: "Mike, why don't you just come clean so we can get this over with?"

"It wasn't me!" I persisted in claiming my innocence.

The detective left the room and came back with a manila envelope containing several photos. He pulled the photos out, laid them in front of me, and began to explain them to me.

"Mike, this is a photo of the damage done inside the trailer. I want you to pay close attention to this one—the photo of the shoe print we found in the kitchen. Now, here's another picture of the shoes we got from you yesterday. See any resemblance?"

As I looked at the pictures, my heart sank! I was indeed busted. There was no denying the evidence before me. I sat there motionless, staring at the pictures and wondered what was going to happen to me.

After a few minutes, the detective broke in, "Mike, why don't you tell me what happened that night?"

I began to lay out the entire story, from the initial plan to who was involved to a step-by-step account of what we did that night.

After I was done, the detective told me, "Wait here." He went and talked with my mom, and then returned to the interview room. "Mike, you're in some serious trouble. We're charging you with breaking and entering and with malicious destruction of property."

I knew my life was over when he said that. All I could think about was me and the trouble I was in. I never gave one thought to how my friend felt, how his parents felt, or how anyone else I had hurt by my actions was affected. I only thought about myself. What I didn't know at the time was that every decision I had made was causing my life to move in a direction, and every direction was leading to a destination. My decisions were getting more and more seriously destructive to my life and future. At the time I thought I was in the worst trouble of my life, but little did I know that I was just starting out on a long journey of crime.

The juvenile court judge I appeared before sentenced me to probation and community service. He told me that any probation violation would mean I would be locked up in the juvenile detention center, of which I also was given a tour. But that was not the extent of the consequences for my actions. At home I was grounded for a long time and only allowed to walk to and from the bus stop.

My friend was surprisingly cordial to me and told me he was still friends with me, which really blew my mind. He even gave me a play-by-play of what his parents did and said when they first discovered the damage I had done to their home. He remembered being very angry at first, but once he saw that his room had not been touched, or his sister's, he actually was not that upset about the frustration his parents experienced over the incident.

The reason he and I got along so well was that we both had a lot of deep-seated pain and anger in our hearts, and we both were rebelling against society and all forms of authority, including our parents. Only, I took it to the extreme. The coping mechanisms I was using to comfort the deep aches in my heart were causing more and more pain in my life, and the consequences were being felt outwardly as well. What was in my heart in abundance was making its way into my personality and my decisions, and it was starting to shape and mold my life.

On the Receiving End

One day as I was walking back from the bus stop in the neighborhood next to our trailer park, I was jumped by two grown men. As I took the trail through the row of pines that separated that neighborhood from the trailer park, I saw two men running right toward me. Before I could react, they tackled me in the snow and proceeded to beat me mercilessly about my head, face, and body.

Blood was everywhere, turning the white snow crimson red. I tried to fight back, but these two guys were pretty big.

Finally they stopped hitting me and got off me and ran as some passersby started yelling at them. I stood up with my face swollen, bruised and bleeding. My adrenaline was running at full capacity, and I was filled with rage! It wasn't so great to be on the receiving end of a crime, but whichever end I was on, as usual, all I could think about was myself. All I could think about was how I could find out who those men were and how I was going to get them back. At that instant, I swore to myself that I would never let anyone hurt me again! I made an inner vow that would set a course for my life into adulthood.

I made my way back home, and my mom freaked out when she saw me walk in the door. I was battered, but not enough to go to the hospital. I insisted that Mom not call the police, either. Years later, I would find out that those men had been sent by someone else to teach me a lesson, as a payback for something I had done.

It wasn't long after that incident that we got the news that my family was being evicted from the trailer park for the damage I had caused in the park, with the incident of the vandalized trailer. I was devastated, because now I felt a lot of uncertainty again. I worried about where we would move. *Will it be somewhere close or somewhere far away?* I wondered. My parents wanted to move away to another city so we could have a fresh start, but all I could think of was, *I am SO tired of moving!*

We ended up moving to a small town east of Grand Rapids. That was a drastic change for me because once again it was a rural town where there were a lot of farms and farmers. Small towns are places where everyone knows each other. We moved into another trailer park near town.

I was enrolled at the local middle school, and my sister Alicia was enrolled at the elementary school. I was the new kid once again and I automatically gravitated toward the "cool" crowd, where I made some friends and some enemies. Because I was the new kid, all the girls took an interest in me, and not all the guys liked that. I guess the girls were tired of looking at the same boys ever since grade school, and I certainly did not mind their interest!

I became close friends really fast with a guy who had similar interests to mine: sex, drugs, and rock and roll. And of course, we loved to fight and prove ourselves as two individuals you did not want to mess with! We weren't the types who were bullies or who looked for fights, but we were ready for a fight whenever there was any opportunity to show what we were made of. (We are still good friends, but we are a little more mature about our activities now.)

One night in particular way back when, I was heading to a party store in town. This party store was known for its ease of access. The alarm system was primitive, even for back then. I had found out that if I put tin foil between the connections in the door and used my high school ID, I could actually pick the lock and get into the party store. Now and then I would sneak in and take a fifth of whiskey or a fifth of vodka or something from the back of the alcohol shelf, and then I'd lock everything back up on my way out. That way, when the store owners came back, they wouldn't see anything amiss and they wouldn't notice the theft for days. When they finally found the empty spot at the back of the shelf where the bottle I took had been, they would have no idea who did it. It could've been an employee or whomever.

With that party store as an easy target, I had a pretty good thing going on. It made me really popular with some of my friends. We didn't have to find a buyer; we didn't even have to pay for our booze. I could just pick the lock on the party store once in a while and grab a free bottle of booze. One night as I approached the store after closing time, I noticed an older guy in the parking lot. Somehow he had found out about my little scam. He was there with a truck, and he was going to break in and haul as much as he could out of the store.

I started to argue with him, telling him, "No, man, you can't mess me up! This is a good thing I have going on!"

We exchanged some more heated words, and it wasn't long before things escalated into a fight. That was okay with me. I was into martial arts at the time, and I knew some taekwondo. I loved fighting! The guy I was about to fight with was considerably larger than I was, and I'll never forget him coming at me. He had a pretty mean reputation, I found out afterward. He took a swing, and I dodged out of his way. Then I grabbed his hair and tripped him. He went face-first into the concrete and lay there moaning.

I turned my back on him and started to walk away, thinking he was out of it. Suddenly, he jumped on my back. The last thing I remember was seeing him take a knife and raise it as high as he could, and then bring it down. He intended to stab me in the neck, but he missed and hit me in the jaw.

I went down hard. The immediate searing pain brought me down face-first, and I didn't know what had happened.

The next thing I knew, I woke up with blood all over my coat; blood was everywhere. I was losing a lot of it, and I was getting weaker. Someone got me into a car, and I wound up at the hospital. I ended up receiving several stitches in my face, and the scar that I have to this day is a reminder.

Of course, the police interviewed me. They wanted to know if I knew who my assailant was. I told the officer I didn't know. (Later on, I found out who he was.) I told the police I couldn't remember what he looked like, either. It was dark out and he had snuck up and ambushed me after I thought he was down for the count. I never saw it coming. I definitely didn't want the police to find him because I wanted to take revenge on him myself. Every day it burned in my heart, the anger that somebody had stabbed me. *One of these days I'm going to get the guy who stabbed me,* I told myself.

One night I was out partying, drinking and smoking marijuana with some friends. We pulled up in front of the party store, the same party store that I was ripping off on a weekly basis. I got out of the car to go inside. I looked around, and lo and behold there was the guy who had stabbed me. He was standing at the counter, about to pay for something.

I went out to the car and grabbed a tire iron, and I waited outside for the guy to come out. As soon as he did, I never gave him a chance to recognize anything—I just hit him as hard as I could in the head and face with the tire iron. He went down. I got on top of him and started to pummel his face and jaw as hard as I could with both my fists, until finally some guys pulled me off him, got me in the car and got me out of there fast.

That night I came home very intoxicated. My sister Alicia remembers that I was walking sideways, basically defying gravity, and talking about how I kicked the guy's butt. She looked at my fists and saw that there were teeth embedded in my knuckles. She pulled the teeth out of my knuckles and put peroxide on my hands while I proceeded to pass out.

Some of my friends and I, we were trouble from the start. We got to know our town's police force rather quickly and rather well. We had a reputation with law enforcement, as well as with our school authorities. One particular time, I remember driving around downtown on a stolen dirt bike with one of my friends. It was an Enduro dirt bike, the type that you can drive down trails as well as on the street. We quickly got into a high-speed chase with the police. We headed for the railroad tracks and wiped out, and my friend got away. I didn't. I got into my first fight with police officers instead. They had to wrestle me to the ground as I cussed and swung my fists and kicked at them. It took them quite a while to subdue me and get me into the back of their vehicle.

Quite a crowd gathered around the scene because it happened right downtown. At the time, I was so proud of the fact that I had fought the police. I landed a punch on one of them and kicked him. I didn't even think about the consequences. I was young and had a lot of pain in my heart, so I just didn't care. They brought me down to the police station and handcuffed me to the wall.

My mom was usually the parent who handled calls from the school or from the police. She came down to the police station. She should have been mad that her son was driving recklessly through town at high speed on a stolen dirt bike. But instead, but she was more upset that the police had handcuffed me to the wall. She couldn't believe her eyes when she saw that. Had she been present at the scene where her son had caused such an uproar not half an hour prior, she would have understood why they had to handcuff me to the wall. I was released into my mom's custody, though, and taken home.

Of course, I lied and told Mom I didn't know the dirt bike was stolen, yada yada yada . . . Lying seemed to be a way of life for me. From a young age I had learned that if I lied, I could cover up what I had done wrong. If I lied, people wouldn't know what I had done. This pattern of lies would haunt me the rest of my life. I have overcome that pattern with God's help, but it can still be a strong temptation at times for me. Lying is an area the enemy has me marked in, so that means it's an area where I need to rely heavily on God's grace.

Being the "Bad Boys"

My friends and I were the guys in middle school that the girls liked because we were the "bad boys." We kept up our tough-guy image at all times. We wore leather jackets. We wore our hair long. We got into all kinds of rebellious things. We had the whole cool persona going on, which caused a lot of fights with the guys we called "the jocks" in school. Some of the farm boys fought against us, too, because they thought we were long-haired punks. We got into many a fight both in school and after school.

About this time in my life, I got heavier into the drug culture because of an older kid I knew who was a well-connected supplier and marijuana dealer. Thanks to him, I would smoke marijuana any chance I got. I remember a friend and I would take these big round cans that cheese puffs came in, and we would cut a hole in the top.

Then we would make a little bowl in there with some tinfoil, and we would poke a hole in the back plastic part and poke a hole in the tin. We would put some weed in there and smoke it and do a bong hit where you fill the can up and then release the thing and suck in all the air.

I remember we would walk to school and smoke joints of marijuana on the way. Then we would eat mints and spray Polo cologne on to cover our scent. We were high at school just about all of the time. I've always been smart in school, and every teacher I ever had told me I was intelligent. But besides being high at school, part of my problem was the homework. I never wanted to do my homework. I figured school was time to do schoolwork and home was time to do what I wanted, so it was very difficult for me to get my homework done. In class, though, I would do my assignments and do them rather well.

I wasn't only a "bad boy," though. I had some other skills, too. I was always a big kid, bigger than the rest of the kids in school. I was head and shoulders taller and bigger muscularly, so of course, the teachers wanted me to play football and other sports. I applied myself at sports (way more than at homework), and I found it was something I was really good at. Excelling in sports got me a lot of attention. It brought me a lot of accolades, and it made the teachers like me. It also made me popular. I ended up being one of those kids who was on both sides of the fence. I had one foot on the stoner side of the fence and the other foot on the jock side. I pretty much got along with both crowds. I've always been good at getting along with people—at least the ones I wasn't fighting with. And even with people who didn't like me, I had a way of winning them over if I wanted to.

I got to know some teachers well, too, and they got to know me. But with my poor choices and poor habits, I ended up on the verge of not making it to high school. In eighth grade, my grades were right on the borderline. When I realized that all my classmates were going to go on ahead of me into high school and I would probably have to stay back in middle school, it finally motivated me to kick it in gear academically. Being held back would have been a *total* social disaster/ catastrophe in my eyes, so I start applying myself to my schoolwork. I actually began to do my homework, and I got my grades caught up to the point where I could finally finish middle school on time with the rest of my friends.

Middle school is a time of huge change in any young person's life, but it was a really tough time for me. I was uncertain/insecure/ hurting on the inside and bad boy/stoner/sport jock on the outside. I didn't know who I was or what I was born for; I was just focused on showing the world I could be a man—except I didn't know what being a man really meant. Like I said, I really didn't have anyone to show me, so I tried to figure it out on my own. That didn't work so well. Sex, drugs, fistfighting and rock and roll don't equal manhood, but I sure thought they did!

They say that middle school is when young people form a worldview and set a course for their lives. Many of their academic habits and social habits are formed in middle school. They say that once kids reach high school, it's hard to change because they are already set in their ways. I believe all that. In middle school, my worldview was forming in a negative direction, to say the least. That time in my life was formative in more ways than one, and my decisions shaped a lot of my future—or misshaped it, to tell the truth. I was becoming set in my ways, and they were ways that led toward a dark and painful destination. They were ways that would cause a lot of pain and damage to a lot of people. Kids who are like I was at that age are the reason the Conquerors do so many school assemblies, to motivate young people to make positive decisions and change their negative ways.

3

My "Baby" and Our Baby

In my last year of middle school, I met Stacey Lang. She was a beautiful girl with gorgeous hair, and we were in opposite classes in school. We would see each other all the time, though, because our classrooms weren't individual rooms. We were in one large room with a divider down the middle. I would sit in my chair in the back of one "room" and see Stacey over there on the other side of the divider. Looking at her, I'd kind of flirt with her. Finally, she and her boyfriend broke up and she became available, so I asked her out. We hit it off, and I began to hang out at her house.

Stacey lived with her mom and her stepdad. Let me tell you, that guy was one scary dude. I'll call him Keith, and he was a big, big man. He was over six feet tall, and he was hugely muscular and had tattoos all over his arms. He had a big, long beard, and he was as mean-looking as they come. Keith had spent quite a few years in the Hells Angels, the notorious motorcycle gang from out in California. I'll never forget the first time I met him at his house. I walked in the door, and two guys were sitting at this table. Keith had his buddy Phil with him, who was even scarier than he was. I couldn't believe it. I thought I had never seen a scarier man in my life than Keith, but then I glanced from him to the other guy—his buddy Phil.

Keith and Phil had served together in Vietnam, and they were both what they call Lurps or LRRP: long range reconnaissance patrol. Lurps were the guys who really excelled at killing the enemy, and they often did things like hanging cut-off ears around their necks as souvenirs. Keith and Phil had volunteered for three tours in Vietnam. When they finished their tours of duty over there, they came back to face a culturally tumultuous time in our country's history. The protests against the war made them feel like outcasts or outlaws. Feeling betrayed by their country, they joined a motorcycle gang.

The criminal activities of motorcycle gangs are well-known. Those gangs are not exactly made up of perfect model citizens, nor law-abiding ones. So here was Keith sitting in the kitchen of Stacey's house with Phil and smoking unfiltered Camel cigarettes. I'll never forget how I walked in with all my bravado, all my toughness, all my bad-to-the-bone attitude and was stopped short at the sight of them. I carried off my big attitude everywhere else rather well. I carried myself in a way that let people know I wasn't somebody to mess with. But all that bravado went flying out the door as soon as I walked into Stacey's kitchen. I took a big gulp and was actually pretty scared. Those two guys just looked at me with this thousand-yard-stare, and Keith's eyes said, *Hmm, so here's the young man who wants to date my daughter...*

That stare was one any boyfriend dreads coming his way from a girl's father. Stacey introduced me to everyone, and I quickly followed her into the living room. We sat on the couch, and I tried to act as proper as I could. Then we went out to the kitchen table and sat down.

By then the big guys had moved out into the garage. Keith called in to me and said, "Hey, come out here! I want to have a talk with you."

Oh, man, here it comes, I thought, *the dreaded talk!* You know, the one between the father and the suitor of his young daughter or stepdaughter.

I stepped out into the garage with him, and he got right to the point. He said, "If you're trying to date my daughter, you better be good to her and you better not use her or break her heart." He pulled out a big bowie knife and added, "Because I will cut your. . . manhood off."

Except he didn't use those exact words. To keep it clean, I'll just say that he made it quite clear what he would do to me if I hurt his daughter or did anything that would disrespect her. I assured him that I had nothing but the purest motives and intent toward his daughter and that I would treat her like the princess that she was.

"Good," Keith said. "Then you and I will get along just fine."

Like One of the Family

I began to get close to Stacey's family after that. It was kind of strange, but Keith became like a father figure to me. My dad had a limited capacity to get close to me. It wasn't because he didn't have the heart or intent to; he just didn't have the capability due to his physical handicap. It impaired him mentally and emotionally, as well as physically, and he didn't have the ability to teach me certain things that Keith could teach me. You can't really teach somebody something you've never done yourself. Keith kind of took me under his wing and taught me things like how to hunt. I had never hunted before in my life. I had fished when we lived back in Port Sanilac, and I had killed just about every small woodland creature I could get my sights on with my BB gun. But with Keith, I got my first taste of real hunting. We went to deer camp, just me with a bunch of men, and we shot some deer.

I managed to bring down some nice venison, and I remember Keith saying to me that first time, "It's customary for a warrior to eat the heart of his first kill." So I proceeded to eat the heart of my first deer!

Keith also taught me all kinds of survival techniques he had learned, but what I loved more than anything was learning to handle his guns—and he had plenty of them. I love going over to Stacey's house and shooting the guns. Shotguns, pistols, rifles, you name it.

There were plenty of guns to be had, and Keith let me handle and fire them.

In my eyes, between the guns and everything else, Stacey's family was a dream family! They were also very liberal, to say the least. They looked at my rebellion and my drinking as normal "teenage behavior." They did not dissuade me from doing it, and neither did Stacey.

Stacey was a different kind of girl than the ones I was used to associating with. She was an excellent student and athletic, too. She had all the smarts and all the looks to make it and be a big success in life. Then she got hooked up with me. Stacey was my first love, for lack of a better term. We hung out together all the time. I told you before that I had had plenty of experience plenty early with the ladies, but with Stacey it was different. She was my girlfriend.

I remember during football season in our freshman year of high school, I would be downtown for practice, and we would take a break at lunchtime. Stacey would come downtown to meet me, and then I'd end up not going back to practice. I fell in love with her, or so I thought at such a young age. Obviously, I didn't have any clue at the time about what love is. We were very sexually active, and I was a self-centered young man who only thought about pleasing himself. Whatever felt good at the time, I did it. I wasn't very faithful to Stacey, either, but she was very faithful to me.

Stacey did not mind my drinking, but she was couldn't stand it when I had been smoking marijuana. I had to hide that habit from her the best I could.

Then there came the day when Stacey believed she was pregnant. I remember we did a pregnancy test, and sure enough, we found out she was carrying our baby. My family was Catholic and raised me Catholic, so my mom had taught me that abortion was wrong. But at the time, Stacey and I thought an abortion was the only way out. We thought that cleaning up our "mistake" through an abortion would be the answer to our problems. We started looking through the Yellow Pages and trying to find a clinic that would do an abortion for us, but

Stacey was already pretty far along. It wasn't going to be easy (at least, it wasn't easy back then).

Mothers Know Best

I'll never forget how my mom found out. I kept all the notes Stacey wrote me in school in the top drawer in my room, and my mom sensed that something was up. (Moms are like that!) She went into my room and read some notes from Stacey to me. Then she took me to run an errand with her, and she brought up the subject.

"Stacey's pregnant, isn't she?" Mom just said right out of the blue.

I looked at her and said, "How'd you know?"

"I snooped around and read one of her notes," she confessed. (She didn't seem very sorry about it, though.)

"Yeah, she is," I confessed.

"Well, what do you plan to do about that?" Mom asked. "You're not going to get an abortion, are you?"

"Mom, I don't know," I said. "We're thinking about it."

"You can't! You can't get an abortion!" she insisted. "That's a life in there, and you *cannot* do it. I'll fight you tooth and nail. I will *not* let you get an abortion. You need to tell Stacey's parents. I'm not going to; I'm going to give you a chance to do the right thing, but you're *not* going to get an abortion."

Now that my mom knew everything, it was actually a huge relief. We hadn't really wanted to get an abortion anyway. Deep down in our hearts, we knew there was a baby in there, too. But the alternative to an abortion was that we had to tell Stacey's parents about the pregnancy, which scared me to death.

I'll never forget the night we took Stacey's mom out to tell her. I'll call her Denise, and she was always good to me. We took the approach of hitting her up first, thinking we would tackle telling Keith after that. We took Denise out to dinner. I had been working as a dishwasher, so I had a little bit of money, which was a big deal for me. We were able to treat Stacey's mom to a really nice dinner. Of course, her mom being wise, she knew something was up.

Stacey kept kicking me under the table the whole time we were eating. She kept giving me this look like, *Go ahead and tell her!*

I'd give her a look back like, *Okay! Okay!* But I couldn't quite work up the guts to get the words out of my mouth.

It wasn't until the drive home that Stacey's mom said, "So, what do you two have to tell me?"

We both looked at her like, *What?*

She repeated herself, "So, what do you two have to tell me? I know you didn't drag me all the way out here and treat me to this nice dinner for nothing. You must have something to say."

Stacey and I sat there mute. When her mom saw that, the first thing she asked was, "Are you pregnant?"

Stacey nodded her head yes, and I thought, *Now it's coming!*

"Okay," Denise said, "what are you going to do?"

"We're going to keep the baby," we told her.

"All right, that's a good decision," she told us, "but we're going to have to tell Keith about this." Then she turned and looked at me and said, "Probably be a good idea if you weren't there when we tell him, Mike."

Then I thought, *Oh no! This will really be bad!*

They dropped me off at my house and went home. A couple hours later, I got a call and Stacey said, "Keith wants you to come over. He wants to talk to you."

I said, "Is he going to kill me?"

"No, no, it's okay," she said.

My parents and I all went over to Stacey's house, and we had a big meeting. Everyone told Stacey and me about the responsibility that we now had and how hard it was going to be for both of us. All the realities of a teenage pregnancy were going to hit us hard and affect our futures. They talked to us about all the pregnancy might mean for us. It was a tough meeting.

Once the shock kind of wore off, though, Stacey and I got a little bit excited because we were going to have a baby. I couldn't believe it—I was going to be a dad! The whole time Stacey was pregnant, I did what any soon-to-be father would do—I waited on her hand and foot. I went through the months of her pregnancy right along with her, and we had a summer baby. In the month of July my daughter, Alexa, came into this world. Her birth was probably one of the greatest moments of my life. I was the first one to hold her. As she was sitting in my arms and crying, I couldn't believe it was real. I was holding my own daughter. I was a dad. It did hit me hard.

Too Much to Handle

Not too long after the birth, things started to change. Stacey had had enough of my wild ways and broke up with me. I tried to stay close to her family, but it just didn't work out. Because of Alexa, though, I would see them from time to time. They were always nice to me, but it wasn't the same. They didn't seem like family to me anymore, which bothered me. I still got to see my daughter whenever I wanted. Stacey never tried to keep me from seeing Alexa, which I was grateful for. But during that time, the gravity of the life decisions I was making, coupled with the weight of responsibility a new child brings, were too much for any young person to handle—let alone an unhealthy one like me. My heart was full of dysfunction and pain, and I had anger and all kinds of things going on inside me. I didn't know what to do under all that pressure. I turned to heavy drug use. Instead of alcohol and marijuana, I started to experiment with cocaine. I did LSD; I did everything I could. My grades started to plummet. By the time I reached tenth grade, I had to leave my regular high school for an alternative school.

One time a friend and I stayed up for three nights in a row partying, drinking, and snorting cocaine. We came to this place of emptiness where I actually felt as if there were a hole in my soul. I had no future, nothing to look forward to. In retrospect, it was a dark time, a very low time for me on the inside, even though on the outside that's not what I portrayed. I portrayed somebody who was confident, somebody who was able to tackle anything life threw his way. I was the consummate bad boy, but it was only skin-deep.

This partying friend and I were both hungry for a new start, a fresh start. That's what people long for when they get themselves into an impossible situation and bring themselves to such a low point that they can't see up anymore. Their first reaction is to run. Run to another place, move away, quit a job, get a new one—whatever it takes. People inherently think that if they run away from their bad situation, they'll run away from 1) the pain, and 2) having to face the pain.

The truth is, you can't ever run away from yourself. If all your problems and all your situations are always everybody else's fault—the government's, the man's, or somebody else's—then you'll be thinking you can escape them by running. You're going to run to another place, another geographical location and find the same problems, though, because you'll eventually find out that the problems were not with everybody else; the problems were right there with *you*.

It's so much easier just to numb your pain and put the blame off on somebody else, never really dealing with yourself. It seemed to me as if my whole life was a life of pain. Oh, yeah, there were great times. I loved my mom and my dad, and I loved my sisters. I even had a daughter whom I loved, but the truth was, I couldn't stand myself. I couldn't stand where I was going, which was nowhere.

In the midst of this dark, depressing time, this friend and I decided we were going to make a change and get a fresh start. We decide we would go to Florida, but we didn't have any money to get us there. We had no jobs and no career, but we needed some quick money quickly, so we came up with the ultimate plan: We would rob a bank!

When we first talked about doing this bank robbery, a couple other people were with us, and they wanted in on it. They were like, "Yeah, let's do it! Let's rob a bank!" But when it came time to carry out the plan, all of a sudden they had a change of heart. Some people talk about doing things, and other people take action. But my friend and I were the type to take action. We were going to take our plan all the way! We borrowed one of his relative's cars, confiscated another relative's blue coveralls (a pair for each of us), and nabbed ourselves a couple rifles. We loaded everything in the back of the car, and we were ready to go!

We had the bank all picked out ahead of time. It was a United Bank in Alto, Michigan. The town we lived in was small, but Alto was smaller yet. It was a rural community surrounded by nothing but farms and one factory that was the town's largest employer. We headed toward our target. I was high on marijuana and had just finished off my last little bit of cocaine. It was going to be a great bank robbery. No one would ever know we did it, and we'd get clean away with it. We would get on an airplane and fly out of Michigan, out of Grand Rapids, out of our trouble, out of our pain, to a new start. We would head down to Florida and get jobs, start over, do things right, be legit.

That's how we talked to each other and how we deceived ourselves, but I think deep in my soul, I knew that my life would be over if we carried out our plan. Deep down, I knew I was about to make one big, bad decision that would forever alter my future. And I was right.

4

Decision of Destruction

Life is a series of decisions and a culmination of our choices. Every decision we make causes us to move in a certain direction toward eventually reaching a destination. We all make many decisions every day. Some are small: *What am I going to wear today? Hmm, the blue shirt and jeans, or shorts? What shoes do I want to wear?* Some are simple choices: *What am I going to eat? Hmm, this refrigerator is almost empty. Looks as if my options are a sandwich or leftover spaghetti.*

Then there are some more serious choices. They don't seem serious at the time; they may even seem harmless. Yet they have an effect on our future because they set up patterns in our lives. They set up a framework we tend to keep following. We come home from school with homework to do and we make a choice: *I could sit down and do my homework, or I could head out with my friends and play video games. Hmm, maybe I'll get to the homework later. . .* Those "little" decisions wind up being like railroad tracks, and we're the train, headed wherever the tracks take us—good or bad.

And then there are life-altering decisions. That one decision, one moment of time, can alter our future for years to come, sometimes even permanently. Take suicide, for instance. Someone who chooses suicide ends the future, and there is no way to turn that train around.

One fall day when I was sixteen, I made a life-altering decision. My friend, whom I'll call Jeff, and I had already decided to run away from it all, as I told you in the previous chapter. But first, we needed some funds to finance our trip, some quick money quick. As I said, it wasn't long before we thought of a quick way to get our hands on some cash. I did some lines of cocaine and we drank some vodka, and then we took his relative's car and nabbed some coveralls, grabbed some rifles and started driving toward Alto, Michigan, to rob a bank.

Let's Do This!

When we got near Alto, we parked the car on the side of the road and followed the railroad tracks that led into town. There were still some leaves on the trees, and it was still kind of warm outside. We had to walk a considerable distance from where we left the vehicle, and when we got to town, a train was sitting on the tracks. We hunched down on the tracks behind one of the end cars. Just a few feet from us there was a small strip of grass, and then there was the street. Kitty-corner across the street was the bank, and across from that was a party store. Directly behind us was a factory. Although it was quite some distance away, I remember feeling nervous, wondering if some factory worker would step out for a cigarette break and see a couple guys crouched down by the train, both dressed in blue coveralls, both carrying rifles.

As we watched the bank across the street, my heart began to race and my adrenaline started to surge. We watched and waited for a time when no one would be in the bank. We didn't want any distractions to get in the way of what we had decided to do, so we wanted the bank to be empty of customers. Finally, only two tellers were inside.

Jeff looked at me and said, "You ready?"

I said, "Yeah, let's do this!"

"All right, on the count of three. Ready? One, two, three . . ."

Jeff and I just sat there, frozen. He looked at me, I looked at him, and we stared at each other for a minute.

"Are we gonna do this? Are we really gonna do this?" he asked.

I said, "Yeah, let's do it!"

"All right, let's count again. One, two . . ."

Before Jeff could say three, I was up and running. He was running right behind me. As we got closer to the bank, I could see the tellers looking at us, trying to figure out what was going on. A look of bewilderment was on their faces, as if they were asking themselves the same question at the same time: *Is this really happening? Are there really two guys coming into our bank with rifles in their hands and blue coveralls on? All the training we went through, all the scenarios we practiced—is one really happening right now?*

It was a surreal moment. We went into the bank and leveled the guns at the tellers. We didn't tell them to get down on the ground like you see in the movies. We had learned that bank tellers are trained to do exactly what robbers say, so we told them, "Don't push any buttons! And don't put any dye bombs in the bag. Just give us all the money—and give it to us now!"

We handed over a pillowcase. One teller, nervous and visibly shaken, was crying. I was nervous, too, looking around inside and out, trying to spot anybody who might observe us and be a witness. After the tellers emptied the four drawers and put all the money in the bag, we grabbed it, and then we yelled, "Get down on the floor now, and *don't* call the cops!"

As soon as they went down, we ran out of the bank. Of course, we knew they'd soon get back up and call the police, so we ran as fast and hard as we could. We ran down those railroad tracks like people running for their lives—which in this case we were. I remember breathing so heavily getting back to the car. We quickly threw the guns in the back and jumped in. Jeff was driving, and he sped off down a dirt road into the woods.

In the Getaway Car

Our first order of business was to get rid of the evidence, so we drove into the backwoods down that dirt road and tossed the guns as far as we could into the trees. I mean, the chance of anyone finding those guns again was remote. A hunter or someone might eventually stumble upon the weapons, but it wasn't an immediate threat, so we just threw the guns into the woods. Then, as we were driving, we took off our coveralls and threw them in the backseat. We would need to get rid of them, too.

We got back on a paved road and started heading toward Grand Rapids, toward Kent County International Airport to make our escape. By then, the adrenaline had kind of subsided and our excitement took over. We were high-fiving each other and yelling, "Yeah! We did it, man! We pulled it off!"

I started looking at the pillowcase full of money and wondering how much was in there. I thought about counting it, but we were busy lighting up cigarettes and still yelling and celebrating, so I figured we'd get to that later. Suddenly, ahead in the distance, we saw several cars coming our way. We got really tense as the first county police officer sped by. *Voom!* Then the next one. *Voom!* Followed by two state troopers. *Voom! Voom!*

They whizzed by us, back toward the bank in Alto. It was at that very moment that the gravity of what we had done hit us, and our mood changed. We got quiet real quick. We kept driving while thoughts were speeding through my head about as fast as our car was going. My mind was going in circles about the decision we had made and the way we had carried it out. It all started to sink in, and I really started to realize what I had done.

There was no going back, though. We couldn't go back into the bank and hand those tellers the money and say, "Oops, we made a mistake. Our bad."

No, we had done it. We had robbed a bank. Those policemen would be at the bank for a certain amount of time, checking out the scene of the crime, but then they'd be out looking—looking for us. I started to think about my family and all the trouble and pain I had already put my parents through, ever since I was a little kid. I thought about policeman coming to their door or ringing them on the phone, and saying, "Come pick up your son from the police station. He's in trouble *again*."

Of all the pain I had caused my family, this was going to be the most painful thing ever, if they found out. There were my sisters Alicia and Christine. My cute little sisters. Would I ever see them again? Would I ever be able to play with them again? And then I thought of my daughter Alexa. All the weight and gravity of the situation were too much for me.

But it was too late to think of those things now. I cleared my mind, and Jeff and I, somber as we were, kept on driving. We pulled over by a Burger King on the way to the airport and dumped the coveralls. We then drove his grandma's car to the airport.

In the Getaway Plane

The Kent County airport is situated in such a way that all traffic has to come down one main thoroughfare. We drove down it and parked the car in the long-term parking lot. We got out and walked inside the airport. This was long before 9/11 and the Homeland Security measures, so we just walked in, a couple of teenagers, and paid cash for two tickets to Florida, no questions asked. We sat down and waited for our plane, and soon it was time for us to board. We boarded a United Airlines flight and got situated.

We had taken all the cash from the pillowcase and stuffed it in our shoes and coats, so it was on us. Sitting on the plane, we started looking out the window, looking at the road to see if any police cars were coming toward the airport terminal a high rate of speed, with lights flashing and sirens screaming. There was nothing in sight, and I thought again, *Man, we've done it. We're getting away with this. We actually did it!*

After a while, we were still sitting there... and still sitting there... and still sitting there. The captain came on the speaker and said that there were some flights coming in, and air traffic was such that we had to wait to take off. So we waited. . . and waited. . . and waited. The delays were all legitimate, I found out later. But the longer we waited, the more nervous I became. *Was it really too good to be true?* I wondered. *Had we really gotten away with robbing a bank?*

The drugs and alcohol were beginning to wear off, and I started thinking again about what we had just done. I mean, this was no playtime. This was the real deal. Some people out there were going to make finding us a very high priority!

All of a sudden, the captain came back on and announced that they had to turn off one engine to conserve fuel, so we heard the engine shut down. That's when my nerves really starting going off the charts. Finally, we started to see planes taking off. One plane left, and then the next, and we were thinking, *Yes, finally, let's get out of here! We're ready!*

Then the captain came back on again and said, "We've run into a mechanical difficulty. We're going to have to go back to the concourse. Everyone's going to have to deplane until a mechanic can fix the problem, and then we'll resume our flight."

Jeff and I were sitting about midway on the plane, a little bit behind the wing. Everybody started getting off, and we were like, "Uh-oh!" But the circumstances of the delay sounded legitimate to us. Plus, we had been listening to the transmissions between the pilot and the control tower over the headphones there in the airplane.

I remember walking down the walkway, looking out the door at the end and seeing these men standing around in suits. For a split second I thought, *What are those guys doing here?* Then it dawned on me that they must be the first-class passengers. *Ah, yeah, that's it,* I told myself as I walked out the door.

Suddenly, the men with suits reached in, drew out their guns, grabbed us and said, "You're under arrest!"

They slammed us against the wall, put handcuffs on us and whisked us off to a back room. By this time, the media had gotten wind of what was going on. The men in suits dragged us down to the airport police station, which was in plain view of everybody, so the news crews were right outside the door as they took all the cash hidden on us and stacked it on the front desk. We were bent over the desk, handcuffed and ready to go.

Lights Out

Since I was still a juvenile, I was whisked out through a back room. Jeff was already old enough to be considered an adult. They took him right out the front of the airport, with cameras everywhere, and they put him in a police car. Off to jail he went.

I was driven to the Kent County Juvenile Detention Facility. This would be my first experience losing my freedom. I remember arriving there and being processed. My head was in a whirl, and I was thinking, *Okay, I'm a juve-. I might have to do some juvenile time, but it won't be that bad.*

I remember getting the county-issued clothes—the jeans and a sweatshirt they gave me. And I'll never forget when they put me in the holding cell. There was a mattress and a "pillow"—or what they called a pillow, anyway—and that was it, besides the toilet. They put me in the cell, and as I heard a big key lock the door, they called, "Lights out."

Even though there were plenty of others in the holding cell, I remember feeling so alone locked in that dark room. It would be the beginning of years of incarceration.

5

Welcome to the DOC (Department of Corrections)

When I turned seventeen, I was transferred to the Kent County Jail. My first experience being locked up in jail was like anybody else's—scary. Anybody who says they're not scared when they walk into jail to stay is lying. Either that or something is wrong with their head.

First, I was put into a holding cell where the conditions were unimaginable. There were about twenty guys in one holding cell. A few had mattresses on the floor to sleep on, but most were just lying down on the concrete, with only a blanket to cover up with. Most the guys were from the streets. Some were homeless. Some were sitting in the corner, staring off into space. The smell was unbelievable.

I was young and scared. I was also on high alert, ready to defend myself if I had to. But to my intense relief, nothing happened that made it necessary. At mealtime, they came around with a cart and started to hand out what they called food. We got a paper bag with a school lunch milk carton in it, a peanut butter or baloney sandwich and an apple. That was my lunch and my introduction to jail life.

After being in the holding cell for three days, I was taken up to a four-man cell block, where I was put in with three other guys. There

I began to learn what it was like to live your life "in the system." Most of the guys I was locked up with had been in the system several times or were heading back to prison.

I remember this one black guy whose name was Grey. Everybody called each other by their last names, so they called me Benson. Grey was an old guy; he was an old-school hustler from Detroit. He was 56 years old, and he was smooth. I liked him. Mr. Grey and I struck up a friendship. We'd sit up until the late hours playing cards and talking trash to each other and to everybody else. Jail is a loud place because there are always open cell blocks up and down "the rock," as they called it. Jail was called "the rock" because it has always been known as a hard place, and back in the 1920s inmates were forced to hammer on huge rocks all day long, hence the nickname "the rock." The nickname from way back then stuck.

Mr. Grey had been in prison several times and I knew I was heading to prison, so I asked for his advice.

"What should I do in prison?" I asked him. "And what should I not do?"

"Mike," he told me, "you got to set an example. You got to show them in there, especially you because you're a white boy. You got to show them brothers in there that you're not a punk."

That's an exact quote. I thought about it and said, "How do I do that?"

He said, "Well, the first blankety blank [that's not an exact quote] who looks at you sideways in any way, you got to punch him in the mouth as hard as you can. You got to beat him down like you're serious."

I took that into my mental cap and said, "Okay, I'll remember that when I get there."

The jail routine was pretty mundane. We got up in the morning and went down to an actual chow hall, which was a big-sized concrete room. We got in line and went up to the window and grabbed our trays. Then we sat down at a four-person picnic table made of stainless steel. Everything in jail was made of steel or concrete. There was nothing comfortable anywhere. Even the mattresses we slept on (if you want to call them mattresses) felt like concrete. They were nothing more than some fire retardant material stuff in a plastic something or other shaped like a mattress.

We spent our time playing cards, and then on some days we would get commissary supplies. If you had people on the outside who would put money into your account for you, they would be able to put in a certain amount so that you could order stuff out of the commissary. You had to order everything you wanted, and they would write on the top how much money you had. You would turn in an order one day, and three days later they would come around and open a slot in your door and hand you your commissary bags.

Commissary day was a big deal in jail because that's when you got your zoom zooms and wham whams. That's prison slang for Hostess Twinkies and potato chips and Kool-Aid and all that kind of stuff. On commissary day, a bunch of grown men turned into little kids as they were waiting for their bags of goodies. That was our big excitement.

Once in a while, they let us out of our cell block to go down to the gym. We could play basketball or lift weights on an old, classic, outdated universal machine. Weights were something I had gotten into at young age. I got my first set of weights when I was 11. I think they were water weights, and I got them for Christmas. I never forgot to lift them every day. Then I got cement weights, and my heroes became Arnold Schwarzenegger and guys like him—big, huge guys. So when I went to jail, I started to work out whenever I could. Of course, I was already bigger than most guys my age, and I figured if I was going to be locked up, I might as well use the time constructively. I began a workout regimen. I would do push-ups and sit-ups. I would take my pillowcase and fill it full of water bottles to make my own weights. I would do everything I could, anything I could, to get myself in shape.

Eventually, my court date came. After a series of legal maneuvers by my lawyer, I was given a 4- to 20-year sentence in the Michigan Department of Corrections. That meant I would do a minimum of 4 years, but I could do a maximum of 20 years. They gave me some parameters that were the determining factors for how long I would serve my time. If I would do everything they wanted me to do—the programming that they would recommend, and staying out of trouble—I would have a chance of getting out after 4 years. The time of my release would be totally up to the Michigan DOC Parole Board.

It was the summer of 1990 that I was in jail, and I remember the day the guard came to my cell and said, "Benson, time to go." I was taken downstairs along with several other guys who were also going to prison. We were shackled up with hand shackles and foot shackles, and then we were loaded into a van.

We were soon on our way to Ionia, a city in Michigan not far from Grand Rapids. Ionia is known for its many prisons. Because of that, people jokingly call it "I own ya." Driving to Ionia in the van to start my prison sentence, we traveled right through the small town where I lived. That was heartbreaking because it was summer and I was a young kid and here I was traveling into an unknown future, going to a place I'd heard so much bad stuff about. I'd heard that prison was a place where people got raped and killed, and I'd heard that all kinds of other horrible things happened there.

My heart just sank to the bottom on the way to Ionia because I knew I would spend at least the next four years and maybe a lot more locked up. I couldn't imagine spending four whole years—the time it takes someone to make it through high school—incarcerated in prison. On the way there, I was imagining all sorts of misery in store for me, but before long, nothing would be left to my imagination. We would arrive and I would walk in and experience it firsthand. I was so despondent.

The van soon approached Riverside Correctional Facility, which was an RD & C. That means reception and diagnostic center. All the young offenders 21 and under went to this particular prison in Ionia. Anyone over 21 went to Jackson State Prison for RD & C. As I entered Riverside with several other guys, the intake workers (the quartermaster and prisoners who worked in the intake area) gave me my ID card. They took my picture and assigned me my number: **209626**. It told me the number of how many prisoners had gone in before me. Then they gave me my state-issued clothes, which we called "the blues" because they're state blues. I was also given a pair of state shoes, and I was taken into a dormlike gymnasium with a bunch of bunk beds to begin my prison experience.

I went through my classification process next, which was a series of tests to find out whether I had an education or not. The court's recommendations were considered and I saw a counselor, and then the recommendation came that I should finish my education and get a GED. I would also need to obtain substance abuse counseling. I would attend AA (Alcoholics Anonymous) and NA (Narcotics Anonymous) meetings, and of course, I would be expected to stay out of trouble.

Leveling Up

In prison, there's a point system where you have a certain amount of points that classifies you into a certain level of security. Classifications are based on a prisoner's personal history and criminal record. Intake workers look at everything about you and assign you a certain level. This has a huge impact on your prison experience because it determines the security where you're at and the programs and activities you can be involved in.

Because of my previous juvenile court history, I could not go into a level 1 facility, which is a minimum security prison. Because I had committed my first felony before the age of fifteen, I probably would never classify for a level 1. There was also an assault risk classification, and I was a high assault risk because of the type of crime I was charged with, in which there were guns involved. If I committed any similar violent types of misconduct, such as fighting or assault, I would be classified to a very high assault risk facility. They give you what's called a misconduct ticket for infractions. When you're a very high assault risk, you can never enter a level 1 prison until you are granted parole. Once prisoners get parole, the state places them in a level 1 facility to await their release, which usually takes a few months. After all, if you have a release date, they've deemed you fit for society, so why not be in a level 1 at that point?

I automatically was classified into a level 2 facility. After classification, every misconduct ticket you get causes a certain amount of points to go on your record. As the points go up, you go up in levels. You could go all the way up to a level 5, which is if you were *really* bad. Level 5 is a super maximum security prison (a supermax). With my level 2 classification, I was sent to the Michigan Training Unit, where my partner in crime, Jeff Thompson, was housed. The Michigan Training Unit is also known as "Gladiator School," which gives you some idea of the atmosphere I was heading into.

To start the journey into serving my 4-year sentence, I was placed in a gymnasium with eighty bunks in it. Eighty guys shared this gymnasium, and it was loud, hectic, and crazy. Eighty guys also shared a bathroom with just one stall and two urinals.

Remember how I told you I had been advised by Mr. Grey back in jail that if I wanted to establish myself in the prison setting, I had to make a killer first impression? He told me I should react with violence toward the first person who looked at me funny or called me a name or anything like that. If I beat the guy up, that would establish my reputation. The other guys would see that I wasn't somebody to mess with, and that would keep me safe.

I came to find out that was true in prison. The more violent you were, the more people tended to leave you alone. One day I was in the bathroom, using the urinal, and the guy next to me looked over and smiled at me. Now, that's not something you do in prison because it can be taken the wrong way. When I finished using the restroom, I turned to him and hit him in the mouth as hard as I could. I knocked him out and left him in a puddle of blood and urine below the urinal.

I hurried up and got out of there so I didn't get caught for fighting, but word got out. You can't do something like that in prison without getting tested, so I got into another fight shortly after that first one. Only this time it wasn't with one person. It was with several, and they were testing me. I successfully fought them off, for the most part, but I got a black eye. The guards knew I had been in a fight, but I wouldn't tell them whom the fight was with, so they put me in "the hole" for fighting. It's the area of the prison where they don't spray for cockroaches, so you have plenty of visitors and friends. I was taken to A Unit, which was the segregation unit where you're separated from the other prisoners and you're not allowed to have any contact with them. They locked me up in an isolation room, which was the policy for guys who were guilty of major misconduct or assault.

Some kinds of misconduct were called bondable misconducts, which meant you went to a court hearing for them, and they would sentence you to toplock. Basically, that means you're locked down except for meals. Either that or they'd sentence you to loss of privileges, which meant you weren't locked down; you could come out, but you couldn't have privileges like going out into the rec yard and things like that.

I went to my court hearing in front of a counselor and was sentenced to 14 days toplock. I was also charged with a major misconduct of fighting. I was told that if I continued on this path, I would be reclassified and sent to a higher level of security, and also that, because of this misconduct, I was already automatically reclassified to a very high assault risk.

It didn't take me long after that to get another assault ticket. I was definitely leveling up fast! Subsequently, I was reclassified from a level 2 to a level 3. MTU is a level 2 facility, so I would be sent to a regional facility in Carson City, which had a level 3 facility and a level 4 facility, along with a level 1 facility outside the fence.

People believe that if they lock a person up, that will change the person's behavior, hence the name "corrections" for the prison system—as in correcting behavior. But removing people from their environment and placing them in prison confinement is not enough to change their behavior. The issues in a person's behavior come from his or her family upbringing and the wounds of the heart, the things on the inside. In order to change a person's behavior—truly change it—you have to change his or her heart, and you have to change his or her perspective on life.

What I found out over time is that you have to change people's perspective on how they view themselves. I was a wounded young man. I still had past hurts inside from my father, and I was still struggling to discover who I was. That's the question every young person is trying to answer. Honestly, it's a question people of many ages struggle with. Like many others, I was asking myself, *Who am I? Why am I here? What's my purpose?*

I still had hope for a future, though, even as I struggled with these questions in prison. Because I was young, they said I had plenty of time to get my life back in order. They said I could serve out my sentence, return to society, and make a life for myself. But obviously, I had a bad perception of myself. I didn't value myself enough or care about my future enough to avoid getting in trouble and getting into these fights. And leveling up to another security classification surely didn't change my behavior in any good ways at all. After I was sent to the level 3 facility in Carson City, my trouble continued.

There are two things in prison that you *do not* want to get involved with if you want to stay out of trouble. You don't want to get involved in gambling, and you don't want to get involved in the drug trade. Those two things are sure ways of getting in trouble. I got involved with the drug trade when I was in prison. We could buy marijuana in prison. The prices were very, very expensive for very, very small amounts, but it was available. I spent a lot of money on marijuana, money that my parents would send to my account for me. Because my parents were middle class, I was considered pretty well-off compared to most of the guys in prison.

As a result of a drug deal gone bad, I got into yet another fight. This time I was put in the hole, and I was reclassified again. This time they sent me to a level 4 facility. In a short amount of time—within two years of being incarcerated—I had gone from a level 2 to a level 4, I had acquired several major misconduct tickets, and I had become heavily involved in drugs in the prison culture. Yet nothing could change my mind about how I wanted to behave. I stubbornly held on to my troubled ways.

Then something dawned on me. I woke up, so to speak, because I figured that if I was ever going to get out of prison, I'd have to change my ways. I finally saw that if I continued this type of behavior, I could very well do 20 years in prison. Just eating the food was enough to convince a person that he didn't want to spend 20 years there! So after I was placed in level 4, I began to toe the line, so to speak. I avoided getting any more major misconduct tickets. I attempted to follow through with my programming. I was finally straightening up. I was going to school and working toward my GED, and I was enrolled in substance abuse courses.

Squeak, Squeak, Squeak . . .

Out of the blue one day, I was told to pack up because I was being transferred. Quite often prisoners will be transferred just like that, for no apparent reason. The one thing that every prisoner with a family wants is to stay in a facility that is close to family. Carson City was quite a distance from my family, and I was told I was going back to Ionia again. I was excited about that until I found out where I was going—the Michigan Reformatory. In the prison systems in Michigan, two prisons are notorious. One is Jackson State Penitentiary, and the other is the Michigan Reformatory, or "Baby Jackson," as it is called. This place was a level 4 facility known for its violence. It's one thing to establish yourself by fighting in a level 2 or 3 facility, but in these level 4 facilities, you can't make a name for yourself or make your mark unless you stab somebody (or worse). People were frequently stabbed in the Michigan Reformatory; people were frequently killed in there. I had heard all kinds of stories, and I was not very happy about going there!

I will never forget my first experience at Michigan Reformatory. Unlike the dormitory settings or the room settings of the previous facilities I had been in, this was an old-school style prison. There were long galleries of six-by-nine cells right next to each other. There were bars as far as the eye could see. I saw that there were two blocks, I-block and J-block, and they were shaped in a big L. When I was placed in my cell, I could look across to the windows and see outside. I saw a wall around the yard, what they call the "rec yard" (short for recreation yard). and it was overcast and gloomy outside. It was a gray day, and there I sat in my cell, hearing the noises of other prisoners talking to each other and yelling at each other.

Then I heard the squeaking noise: *squeak, squeak, squeak*. It started to get louder. I didn't have what they call a hawk, which is a small mirror. I would learn that having a hawk is very valuable in places like that. You could stick it outside your bars and look down the hall to see what was coming your way or what was going on. Since I didn't have a hawk yet, I just lay down on my bunk and listened to the *squeak, squeak, squeak* getting louder and louder. Then, right in front of my cell, two guards passed by pushing a gurney. On that gurney was a body bag, and it was full. Someone was in the body bag—someone who had just perished.

That scene is forever stuck in my head. I knew right then and there that I was in a place where life didn't matter, where people didn't care about you or your well-being. A person could die or be murdered, and he would be wheeled out in a body bag on a squeaky old gurney, and that's the last anyone would hear of him. Life would go on as usual for everyone else.

6

Doing the Unthinkable

The gravity of where my life was going had started to weigh heavily on me. It started to hit me really hard, which actually stopped me from hitting anyone else hard. Believe it or not, in all my time at Michigan Reformatory, I never got into one fight and I never stabbed anybody. I just kept to myself and kept out of trouble. I guess by this time my size was paying off. I had been weight training for quite a while now, and I was getting pretty big and strong. I was also pretty quiet.

I was in the Michigan Reformatory for a total of seven or eight months. I got my GED while I was there, and my high school diploma equivalency certificate said that I had graduated from Hilltop High School (because Michigan Reformatory is on a hill). I had another classification hearing after that, and my level was reduced from level 4 back down to level 3. I didn't know where I was going to be sent this time, but I knew any place would be better than this place. Low and behold, I was sent right across the street, back to where it all started, the Michigan Training Unit.

Once I got back to MTU, I met some people who would forever change my life. I got to be friends with a guy named Chris. Chris was a cool guy, in my estimation. He was built like an athlete and liked to play volleyball, which I was into big-time in prison. And he liked to play our kind of volleyball—full contact. Things tend to get a little rough behind bars.

Chris and I hung out a lot. We worked out and lifted weights together. We were the same personality, type A, but quiet and reserved. There was this one thing that always bothered me about Chris, though. Whenever he got to talking to me, he'd always be talking about Jesus. He'd say things like, "Mike, don't you know that Jesus died for your sins? Don't you know that He died so that you could have life abundant and life eternal?"

Chris would always be witnessing to me about the Lord Jesus and the Bible and how we must be born again. Then he'd start adding things about the Holy Spirit. I wasn't having anything to do with that kind of talk at the time. After all, I had been raised Catholic. I knew all the stories about Jesus, I knew about Moses and the ark and Noah and the Red Sea splitting. . . I knew all that stuff. I had been to catechism when I was in school, and I had been sprinkled when I was a baby.

I told Chris more than once, "Nah, I don't need it, man. I'm good to go. Me and God, we down—we down like four flat tires."

Something bothered me on the inside whenever Chris would talk to me about that Jesus stuff, but I don't think it was so much what he said. It was the fact that Chris had a peace about him that I couldn't quite put my finger on. He was always laid-back, and he had a smile on his face all the time.

Then there was Chris's friend Bible Jim. Everybody called him that because he always walked around with a Bible in his hand. He always had a big smile on his face, too, and he was forever high-fiving everybody. He was so friendly that it irked me. It rubbed me the wrong way because here I was trying so hard to find out what the meaning of life was, and I was in such a rough spot in my life, and these guys just went around looking as if they were having the time of their lives. I kept thinking, *How can anybody be happy in a place like this? I can't believe these guys!*

I'll never forget one time when Chris and I were playing volleyball, as usual. He was really competitive, as much as I was (not easy), and he and I would get heated sometimes. I remember I went up for the ball this time when Chris wasn't looking. I spiked it right in his face on purpose, and he knew I had spiked it in his face on purpose, and he got extremely angry. He actually started to curse me out.

I started laughing, saying, "Ha-ha, some Christian you are! Yeah, you're talking all that Bible stuff, all that Jesus stuff, and there you are, cursing at me. You're no different than anybody else!"

Chris stomped off the court, and I felt good, like I had really shown him something. But I'll never forget how a few hours later, I walked back into the unit and Chris came out of the showers and walked up to me with his head down.

"Hey, Mike," he said, "I want to apologize to you."

"For what?" I asked.

"For cursing at you out there," he said. "That was wrong of me. I shouldn't have done that. Not only that, but I don't know what's wrong with me to ruin the witness of Jesus like I did. I'm just very, very sorry. Will you forgive me?"

When he asked if I would forgive him, my heart felt as if it were being stabbed. My guilty conscience was telling me that I was the one who had caused the problem. I knew I had really pushed Chris's buttons. Looking calm on the outside, I told him, "Yeah, sure." On the inside, though, I was in knots. That moment was a moment that would impact the rest of my life. Chris sowed seed into my life right then that lay dormant for years. One day, though, it would come to fruition. It would just take a while. Right then, I was just trying to survive another day in prison, another day at MTU.

A New Designation

Not long after that, Bible Jim convinced me to go to one of their Protestant services. That was a big deal in prison because at intake, the state would stamp on your ID C for Catholic, M for Muslim, or P for Protestant, and you had to go to those designated services. I was stamped C for Catholic, so if I was going to a service with Bible Jim, I would have to change my designation. It was a bit of a hassle to change it, but I did the unthinkable—if my parents ever found out, I'd be in for it. I changed my C to a P for Protestant anyway so I could check out the service Bible Jim was telling me about.

The service was down in the MTU auditorium, and it was like no service I had ever been to. I was used to all the ritualistic stuff: kneel down, stand up, kneel down, sit down, stand up . . . I was used to the liturgy being quiet, somber and formal. When I walked in with Bible Jim and saw the music blaring and the guys talking to each other and shaking hands, I didn't know how to react. Everybody was saying "Hey" and calling each other Brother—Brother Bob, Brother Tom, Brother Chester, Brother so-and-so. Everybody's first name seemed to be Brother.

This was all strange to me, so I kind of sat in the back with Bible Jim and a couple other guys from the unit. Then the worship started, and the music was upbeat. People were raising their hands in the air and praising the Lord and all this other stuff, and I was feeling very uncomfortable. It wasn't anything like what I had experienced in church before.

Then a man came up to the stage and began to preach a message. When he started talking, something about him really touched my heart. As he began to speak, I could feel an electricity in the auditorium. It seemed as if his whole message was directed right at me. Only he wasn't talking about superficial things. He wasn't telling me how bad I was and how wrong I was and how I needed to change my ways, how I needed to get right. He didn't say any of the obvious things that I already knew deep in my heart. He spoke right to my heart. It was the weirdest thing.

I knew something was going on inside me, but I wasn't sure what to do with it, especially in that environment. You have to understand that in the prison world, there's a stigma attached to church and church services. The worst person in the prison world is anybody who has committed pedophilia. You can be a robber, a murderer, a druggie, a petty thief, or whatever, and there will be a code of so-called honor among criminals. One thing that is not tolerated in prison, though, is a child molester. This church seemed to have a stigma among the criminal element as the kind of place where that kind of guy hid out. There were a lot of pedophiles and the like in the room. All this was going through my mind as I was scanning the guys and listening to this minister and trying to decide how to react to everything.

Then the minister gave a call. He said, "If anybody wants to accept Jesus as their Lord and Savior, please come forward."

I didn't know what was coming over me, but again, I found myself doing the unthinkable. My heart was overriding my head, and before I knew it I was up out of my seat. With tears in my eyes, I was standing there at the front, making a decision to make Jesus the Lord of my life. Afterward, Bible Jim and everybody came around me to say congratulations.

No sooner did I get over the emotion of the moment and walk outside the doors when the reality hit me. I mean, all I could think was, *What are all the other guys in here going to think of me now? What will happen to my tough-guy reputation that I've been building for so long?* These were the things that were weighing heavy on me. Before I knew it, I had chalked it all up as some kind of emotional experience or something that had happened in the moment. Sadly, it took almost no time at all for me to go right back to my old ways.

A Flop or a Free Man?

It was at that time that I got connected with some organized criminal activities. I worked at the recreation department, and I knew some guys in the prison who were good at smuggling marijuana inside. Through my connections in the rec department, I found even better ways to smuggle marijuana in, and we got involved in doing that a lot. Smuggling marijuana into a prison is an extremely lucrative endeavor because the price for marijuana is quite a bit higher on the inside than what it is on the streets. When you've got the weed, everybody wants to be your friend, of course. And when you've got the weed, they call you "the man." That's good and that's bad, because there're a lot of other people who become your enemies when you're heavily involved in all that.

I was doing this smuggling under the radar, so to speak, because by then I had become a "model prisoner." I was getting close to seeing the parole board, and I did not want to mess that up. After seeing the parole board one time, they had given me a 12-month continuance, or what they called a "flop." That meant, "Not this time, buddy. You're going to have to stick around for another 12 months!"

I was getting toward the end of that 12-month flop, and finally I went before the parole board. And they gave me a parole! I will never forget walking out the gates and tasting freedom for the first time in five years. It was surreal, as if I were in a dream. I felt such a sense of relief that I can't even describe it. As I looked back on the prison, I swore I would never go back!

7

History Repeats Itself

After being released from prison, I had a desire in my heart to do things the right way. Somehow, I knew that my life was meant to be successful and that one day, my deepest desire, my greatest dream would come true. It wasn't a dream of becoming a successful businessman or having millions of dollars; it was a dream of having a family. I wanted to settle down, get married, and have kids. The way I was brought up was not ideal, even though my mom and dad loved me very much and did the best they could. But deep in my heart, I knew that family life could be a lot better than that. I wanted to experience that reality in a home of my own.

While I was in prison, I did a lot of things to improve myself. I worked out all the time to get in shape physically. I got my GED. I did everything I could to set myself up for success when I got out of prison. The day I walked out those prison doors, the day I was released, I thought everything would be different. But some things inside me remained the same. There was one area of my life I had never dealt with in prison—the issues of my heart. The pain and wounds from my childhood were still there. All the damage I had caused my daughter Alexa and myself was still there. The shame of bringing reproach on my family name also remained.

Still, once I got out, I tried my best to make things work this time around. I tried to visit with my daughter Alexa, and it was tough at first. Stacey was very skeptical. She wanted me to visit Alexa in a very restricted environment, with someone monitoring our visits closely. I agreed to do that, though, because I was willing to do whatever it took to see my daughter. Stacey had moved on with her life and had a boyfriend, and I was moving on, too, trying to piece my life back together, but with Alexa in it.

When I was first released, I lived with my mom and sisters, but I wanted to get out of there as quickly as I could. (My mom and dad had separated, and he was living in Florida with my grandma, which would come in handy for me before long.) I wanted to be independent, be on my own, in a big way! I remember going to my first job interview after my release. They looked at my application and noticed that there was a considerable gap in my employment history.

"What about that gap, Mr. Benson?" they asked me.

I jokingly said, "Hey, you know, I was at Penitentiary Technologies trying to get an education."

I thought it was kind of funny, but the interviewer didn't.

"Sorry, we can't hire you," I was told.

Same thing at the next job interview: "Sorry, we can't hire you."

I eventually found employment, but all the rejection I suffered in the process took the negative things I had hidden down in my heart and brought them back to the surface again. With all the pain came the anger and rebellion. I went headlong back into a life of drugs and alcohol, partying, and eventually crime. The drugs and alcohol were just a mask, a futile attempt to medicate my pain. I knew they weren't very effective, but they were all I seemed to have.

After two short years of being free, I was in trouble with the law once again, and no wonder. I had hooked back up with Jeff, my accomplice in that first bank robbery. When people around the little town we lived in saw us back together, they knew it spelled trouble. The two of us went back into crime in a big way. We were breaking into houses and stealing guns, coins, or whatever we could get our hands on. We were selling the guns for money. We were doing drugs. We were doing cocaine. We were smoking marijuana. We were doing acid. We were killing ourselves and our futures.

Stealing a Joyride

Jeff and I were doing drug deals all over the place, in downtown Grand Rapids and in Detroit. One time, we were at his mom and stepdad's house. They rented a little apartment, and above them lived a very large man who would come home every night and pass out on his couch. He had a nice car, a big, fancy one. Jeff and I were tripping on LSD, and he dared me to go up there and take the guy's car keys so we could take his car for a spin.

You could hear this guy when he came in, and you could hear his TV. You could even hear him snoring when he was asleep on the couch. I remember walking up the stairs and going in his front door. He had left it unlocked. There he was, sleeping, and I saw his keys lying right next to him. Sneaking over beside him, I was really tense, really wound up. LSD had heightened all my senses. But I grabbed the keys, pulled them all together slowly and quietly, and walked out the door.

Jeff and I took his big, fancy car. We had a bunch of marijuana we wanted to sell, so we headed downtown and met up with a couple drug dealers we knew. Then, when we were driving to meet another contact, we got pulled over by the Grand Rapids police. Both of us were on parole, and the guy we had in the back also had a criminal record. Besides that, Jeff had a bunch of marijuana stuffed in his pants, and we were tripping on acid. Everything was working against us.

Oh man, this is it, I thought. *I'm going back to prison.*

I don't know how or why, but the police just had us sit in the car while they asked us questions. They ran the car, but since it was about 2:00 a.m., the car's owner hadn't woken up yet and discovered his car was missing. The car hadn't been reported as stolen, so the police let us go.

I can't believe it! I thought. *That was a really narrow escape!*

By the time we got home it was about 6 a.m., and we didn't want to drive in and park the guy's car back in his parking spot. For some reason he might be up looking out the window. If he were to see us getting out of his car, we would be busted. Instead, we parked it a few parking lots down, thinking he would figure he parked it there by mistake. He had been drunk a different night and had parked it in the wrong spot, so maybe he would think he did the same thing again.

Once we parked his car and got out, we thought we had gotten away with our joyride. Then two weeks later, when I was about to head home from a friend's house, I got a call from my mom. She was hysterical (and I don't mean funny).

"The police were at our house looking for you," Mom said.

"For what?" I asked.

"They said grand theft auto," she replied, very upset. "They have a warrant out for your arrest."

I thought, *Oh man, here we go. I'm going to go back to prison forever.*

At that time in the 1990s, there was a big push in Michigan to be tough on crime. They had come out with a law called the O'Hare Law, which said that if you were on parole and committed a felony, you had to finish the tail end of your sentence that you were presently on parole for. I had been sentenced to 4 to 20 years in prison, so my "tail" was 20 years. That meant if I was arrested for this car theft, brought into court, and convicted, I would first have to finish the 20-year sentence, and then begin whatever other sentence they would give me on top of it. What would have been a 1- or 2-year crime for our stolen joyride would turn into 20-plus years.

Jeff and I had a decision to make. We could turn ourselves in and face the law, face the justice system, take whatever punishment came our way, and deal with it, or we could go on the run as fugitives. Taking responsibility was not anything I was used to doing, and the thought of spending more than 20 years of my life in prison didn't appeal to me. There was only one choice I could see. We decided that we were going to make a run for it.

A Crime Spree Road Trip

Jeff and I got ourselves a gun and found a ride into Belding. We were going to be there for just one night, so we headed down to a local bar. We had a bunch of money on us from our prior criminal activities, and we began to drink heavily. We played some pool and stayed until the bar closed. We were the last ones to leave. As the barmaid was closing up the place, Jeff and I had a "brainstorm." We decided we would rob the bar, take the barmaid's car and get out of the state. We went back inside and tied her up. Nervous and extremely frightened, she began to shake, but I wasn't too concerned about her problems or anyone else's right then. When we took her car keys, she pleaded with us not to take her car, but we did it anyway. We took all the money out of the cash register, grabbed her purse while we were at it, and grabbed a bunch of bottles of booze.

Loaded in more ways than one, we climbed in her car and left. We headed out of town at a high rate of speed. We went downtown to a motel in Grand Rapids, spent the night, got up the next morning, hopped in her car and headed out of state. We made our way south, heading to where all the criminals go—the State of Florida.

We didn't have a plan. We were just on the run, living every day for the day, with no thought of the future. We pulled a couple other robberies on the way south. We stopped in the little town of Lebanon in Indiana. It was October, and the weather was typical for a fall day in the Northeast, rainy and windy. We stopped at a local bar and started playing pool and drinking heavily again. We were getting low on cash, so we knew we needed to pick a new target. Once we left the bar, we began driving around and looking for a gas station to hit up.

We soon spotted our target, a Shell gas station. We parked the car, and I went in with the gun in my waistband. I ducked into the bathroom and made sure the coast was clear. When I came out, I stuck the gun to the gas station attendant's head and told him to open the cash register. Frightened, he kind of froze in place, like a zombie. Jeff came running in a couple seconds later and just ripped the cash register right off of the counter and threw the whole thing in the backseat of the car. We left the attendant at the counter with his head down like we told him to keep it if he knew what was good for him. We ran outside, got in the car and proceeded out of town, again at a high rate of speed (as usual).

Unbeknownst to us, this particular gas station was directly across the street from the Boone County Jail and the Boone County Sheriff's Office. Bad choice! We had not noticed it at the time because the power was out on that other side of the street. But it turned out this gas station was not your ordinary gas station. It was owned by the former sheriff of Boone County. We later learned that when the dispatch got the call about the robbery, nobody could believe that someone would hold up that particular gas station.

Driving in the dark, we headed down some back roads, traveling mighty fast even though it was raining heavily. Somehow we made it to another little town not far from Lebanon and noticed at that point that there was a truck following us. We turned down one road, and it turned with us. We turned down another road, and it stayed on our tail. Finally, we pulled into a parking lot.

"I'll see who this is following us," I told Jeff as I got out of the car. I walked behind the car, and just at that moment I saw this guy get out of the truck's driver seat. In the next instant, I saw the police patch on his coat.

The guy pulled out his gun, pointed it directly at me, and said, "Hold it right there."

I put my hands up, smiled, turned around and ran back to our car. I jumped in, slammed the door, and said, "Let's go! Let's go! It's the police!"

We exited the parking lot with tires screeching. When we turned onto the main road, it looked like Christmas outside. All these police vehicles had their lights flashing, ready and waiting for us. We started a high-speed chase and put quite a gap between ourselves and the law enforcement vehicles at first. Due to the weather conditions, they weren't driving as fast as we were. However, we were driving so recklessly that we couldn't hold it on the road for long. We ended up crashing the car into a ditch. Indiana cornfields have huge ditches, larger than your average roadside ditches, and we lost control of the vehicle in the rain because of our high rate of speed.

Jeff and I abandoned the car and took off on foot through the cornfields, running as fast as we could. We were running in mud that was ankle deep, and all we had on were flannel shirts. We didn't have heavy coats or anything like that to protect us from the elements, so it wasn't long before we were both a freezing, muddy mess, but we kept running.

Soon we heard the search helicopter in the distance. I knew from being locked up in prison for years already that the police always set up a perimeter when searching a certain area. I knew that if we could get outside the police perimeter, we had a chance of getting away. We finally made it near a farmhouse and saw two police cars driving toward each other on the road, shining their lights into the field near where we were. We hid down in the grass, and as soon as the police cars passed each other, we ran across that road and continued on into the next cornfield.

After running for probably an hour straight, we could tell that we were quite a distance away from the police perimeter. We could see the helicopters in the distance, still searching. We found a camper in the backyard of a farmhouse, and we went inside. Shivering and freezing in that dark camper, we contemplated our next move.

Jeff was feeling pessimistic. "What are we going to do? We're freezing to death!" he complained.

"You want to turn yourself in?" I asked him. "You go ahead! I'm out of here!" There was no way I was giving myself up, ice cold or any other way.

I left the camper, and Jeff followed me. We headed into a small town nearby and started searching for keys in vehicles. We figured that out in the country in small-town Indiana, surely people wouldn't be as wary as they were in the city about leaving their keys in their cars. The light of dawn started coming, and we knew that if we didn't hit the road fast, it wouldn't be long before we were caught. I remember seeing a bunch of vehicles in the parking lot next to a co-op building, and I leaned into this one red co-op truck and reached over to the ignition. *Bingo!* Keys!

I yelled to Jeff, "Hey, there're keys in this truck!"

He looked at me and said, "Uh-huh, sure."

I turned the ignition, and then he got a big smile on his face.

We hopped in the truck, went to a gas station, filled up the gas tank, grabbed a pack of cigarettes and hit the highway. Nervously, we looked at every vehicle that went by. Lebanon was only twenty minutes outside Indianapolis city limits, so we soon made it into the big city of Indianapolis. We booked a hotel room and took hot showers that night. The next morning when we woke up, we stood on the balcony of the hotel and watched the co-op truck for a while just to make sure that the police hadn't tracked us in the night. We were suspicious of them setting up an ambush or waiting and just tailing us to find out who was driving the stolen vehicle. We went across the street to a store and bought some new clothes. We each got some fresh shirts and some sweatshirts. Then we got in the truck and left of town.

Once we crossed the Indiana state line into Kentucky, we thought, *We're home free! We made it out of there!* We knew there would be a nationwide manhunt for us, but we knew the statewide hunt in Indiana was the immediate threat, so once we crossed that border, we felt a huge relief. From there, we continued down our usual path of partying and drinking and stealing and robbing.

Traveling Salesman

In Tennessee, Jeff and I "decided" to go our separate ways. Unbeknownst to me, Jeff had put a call in to his family members and had told them I abandoned him at a truck stop in Tennessee. He then told me that he convinced them to drive down and meet with him. He said he planned to get some money off of them. Several hours later, when he saw their car approaching, he told me to get down and stay down because he had told them he was alone. If they knew I was with him, he said, they probably wouldn't help him out with any cash. So I stayed in the truck with my head down for quite a while. About an hour later, I finally looked up. To my surprise, their car was gone—along with Jeff! He had headed back up toward Michigan with them.

I continued on my way south. Eventually, I made it to where my dad and grandmother were living in Florida. I stopped at a Florida rest area before I got to their place and wiped the truck down of all fingerprints. My dad came and picked me up, so I left the truck right there. Dad never knew about it; I told him I had been dropped off at the rest area.

I stayed with my dad and grandma for two or three weeks. While I was there, I answered an ad in the paper for a traveling sales job. It involved selling cleaning chemicals door-to-door. I went to a hotel to meet with the interviewer, and she said to go pack up all my stuff, come back in a couple hours and be ready to hit the road.

I began selling door-to-door all over Florida, and I did it pretty well. We'd get up in the morning and come in for a sales meeting, and then we'd go out in different crews in different vehicles. We had different team leaders, and we'd go out into what we called territories. We'd drive around a territory either solo or in pairs, depending on if we were training new sales people. If you were really good, you got to go out solo. As I was being trained, I would shadow somebody with more experience. We'd knock on a door and someone would answer.

"Hey, how're you doing today?" we'd ask. I'd notice that the person had a dog, and I'd say, "My dad (or somebody) raised that type of dog," and it would start a conversation. We'd do anything we could to win someone's trust and make a sale.

I moved up in that organization pretty fast, and I got to be one of their top salespeople. It was basically a young person's dream job. We'd sell during the day and party all night. I spent about three months traveling, partying and selling stuff door-to-door, and several times I ran into law enforcement because we'd be knocking on doors in a wealthy community. Somebody would call the police because we were soliciting in their neighborhood, and the police would come find us. I'd give the officers a fake name, a fake birth date, and fake information, and they'd warn us, "Don't sell anything around here. There's no soliciting in this neighborhood." Then they'd leave. We'd go wait down the block for a half hour or so and then continue selling.

It didn't bother me whenever I saw law enforcement pull up, because they didn't know who I was. They didn't have my picture all over the place. If I had been in Indiana, I would have had good reason to be nervous about it, but I figured since I was in Florida, I was good to go. That held true until one day when this particular officer pulled me over. He was an older gentleman, probably with a lot of police experience. He asked me to sit in the back of his car, which I thought was odd. But he didn't put me in cuffs or anything, so I cooperated.

Something inside of me said, *All right, just sit in the car like he says because he's not putting you in cuffs. You don't want to start running and alert him and get the whole police department chasing after you.* So I sat in the back of the police car and gave him the same spiel as usual, with fake information. Suddenly, he put his car in drive and started driving off.

"Wait a minute—what are you doing?" I asked.

"You can sue me later," he said, "but something in my gut tells me you're not telling me the truth. You're not who you say you are, so I'm going to run you in and we're going to do a print check."

I sat in the back of the car with my heart sinking because I knew my life was over. I mean, I knew it. I was busted. I knew they would find out who I really was. They'd find out that I was wanted in Michigan. They'd find out I was a parole absconder. Eventually, they'd trace me back to the armed robbery in Indiana. My life was *over.*

They ran me into the Sarasota County Jail and ran my prints. Sure enough, they came back down to the holding cell and said, "Mr. Benson, there are a lot of people out there who want to talk to you." The officer who had brought me in had a big smile on his face as they closed the gate on me.

At that moment, I knew I would spend the rest of my life incarcerated behind bars.

8

Indiana Intervention

They processed me into the Sarasota County Jail and moved me into the maximum-security cell block to await my first court appearance. I went in completely depressed and angry at where my life was going. I got on the phone to call home collect, and I told my mom where I was and what was going on. She was heartbroken to hear it, of course; I could hear it in her voice. But she also said she was glad that I wasn't on the run anymore.

To make matters worse, naturally some of the other cell inmates wanted to test the new guy, and I was the new guy. Somebody came up to me and said, "It's time for you to get off the phone."

I looked at the other phones that were there with nobody using them, so I knew it wasn't because I was taking up anybody's phone time. I knew they were testing me to see if I were going to fold up and get off the phone. I looked the guy square in the eye and told him to you-know-what off, and I continued my already difficult conversation.

The guy went over and said something to his buddies, and another of them came over with him this time. One of them reached up and hung up the phone on me. Now it was them or me.

I knew that there's no such thing as a fair fight in jail, and I knew I'd probably end up getting jumped by all the guys at once, so I took what I figured was my only option. I grabbed the first guy I could get my hands on so I could do as much damage to him as possible before they got to me. I got him in a half nelson and slammed his head as many times as I could into the nearest set of bars. I kept slamming his head into those bars with all my might, as hard as I could, until the other guys jumped on me. Then I balled up in a ball on the floor while they kicked me and beat me.

The officers came into the cell block and started yelling, "Break it up! Break it up!" Finally, all the guys got off me. There were several officers in and around what was called the bull pen; they hadn't all entered the cell block because it was maximum-security block that contained high-level, violent offenders. (The officers never came inside unless they were in riot gear.) They were yelling for me to come on into the bull pen, which was a cage right in front of the cell block door that helped make sure only one prisoner could exit at a time.

I got up with my nose bleeding all over the place, and I remember all those guys standing there staring at me like they couldn't believe I had even gotten up. I looked behind me, and the first guy I had grabbed was lying in a pool of blood. I had bashed his head against the bars so many times that he wasn't even moving. I walked out ranting and raving at the rest of them, taunting them for all I was worth.

"Yeah, you couldn't even knock me out," I yelled. "That was weak, man! You're a bunch of wussies!" (I added a few other choice comments on my way past them, but I won't repeat those here.)

The officers finally got me to come out into the bull pen. I had to get there on my own because they hadn't come inside. They took me down to the infirmary and assigned an officer to drive me over to the local hospital to have my nose checked out. The X-rays at the hospital showed it was broken. They brought me back to the jail and put me in the INS (Immigration and Naturalization Service) detention block, where a bunch of people who were in the country illegally were waiting for their court hearing. I was placed in a cell with a Colombian drug dealer who was awaiting extradition back to Colombia. He and I got along very well, so nobody got hurt after that.

Which Way to Go?

Soon I was taken to my Florida court hearing. The judge basically recognized that I was a fugitive from the State of Michigan and made it a matter of public record that I was being held at the jail until they could figure out which state authority they would release me to. At this court hearing, I found out the full extent of the charges pending against me in Indiana. I was wanted in that state for armed robbery, fleeing and alluding police officers, car theft, vehicle theft, and transportation of stolen property across state lines, which is a federal charge. I also found out I was wanted in Michigan for armed robbery, kidnapping, and auto theft. Those were the charges that stemmed from robbing the bar and violating my parole. (We hadn't actually taken the barmaid with us; the kidnapping charge was due to the fact that we had tied her up and prevented her from leaving, which is considered kidnapping.) It was not good news that not only did I have all those charges in Michigan and Indiana against me, but that I now also had federal charges against me.

I left the courtroom with a broken nose, two black eyes, and deep depression for company. I was going to spend the rest of my life incarcerated. Shortly after the court hearing, I was told that a federal marshal had arrived to see me. I went into the interview room, and this federal marshal slid two pieces of paper in front of me.

"If you sign this paper," he explained, "you will be released into the custody of the State of Michigan. Officers from Michigan will come to pick you up, and you will be transported to a Michigan Department of Corrections facility, where you will await your parole hearing. Then they will release you to other authorities to face charges for the crimes you have committed." Then he pointed to the other piece of paper. "If you sign this one, you will go to the jurisdiction of the county in Indiana where you committed the armed robbery."

In my own natural thinking, I figured there was no way I wanted to go back to Indiana, because by this time I had found out more about the circumstances surrounding the armed robbery of the gas station directly across from the county jail. I found out just what a dumb target we had picked. This gas station was two blocks down from the state police headquarters and across the street from the county jail. We had caused a lot of trouble by robbing it so brazenly and by leading several state and county agencies on a high-speed chase. Then we caused them some embarrassment by escaping from their perimeter even though they had helicopters and everything searching for us. We had proceeded to steal a vehicle and flee the state, and we had gotten away with it. With all that against me, the last place on the face of the planet that I wanted to go back to was Indiana. I figured that they would bury me under some facility there and name it after me as a memorial of what would happen to criminals stupid enough to do what we did in their state and county.

I have no earthly explanation for what happened next, but for some reason, this federal marshal began to explain to me how I needed to take care of those charges in Indiana first. He wasn't coercing me or anything like that, but he was making an argument for signing the papers to go to Indiana.

I remember thinking in my head, *No way! I'm not going to do it!* But something deep in my heart was telling me that I should sign the paper to go to Indiana. It made no logical sense at all, yet I had this gut feeling that Indiana was the way to go. I didn't know it at the time, but God was definitely intervening in the situation. When I signed that paper, it turned out to be a pivotal moment in my life. I could not see it, but I was at a crossroads and God had a plan for my life. He was working in my behalf to set me up for the future He had planned for me, which I knew nothing about—yet.

As my pen slid across the Indiana paper and I put my signature on it, I remember asking myself, *What are you doing? Are you STUPID? Is there something wrong with you?*

Once I had signed, the federal marshal said, "Well, now we'll see what happens. Michigan has first dibs on you, so they could supersede this with the parole thing, but hopefully you'll be able to go to Indiana and get these other charges squared away."

Back in my cell, my head started reeling. I was kicking myself, unable to believe I had signed that paper to go to Indiana. But now it was done.

Shocking Treatment

Certain laws govern the state transfer of prisoners. There is the interstate agreement on detainers, and there are also laws pertaining to the jurisdictions that are holding fugitives. These laws help keep county jails from overflowing with fugitives from other states. Florida gave other jurisdictions 15 days to come pick up prisoners. If no one came for me within 15 days after I signed the paper, I would be released regardless of the charges held against me (unless it were a capital murder charge, which it wasn't). I got all the way up to day 14, and I even got my hopes up a little (okay, maybe a lot), but on the fourteenth day, one of the sheriffs came down and told me I was leaving. Some officers from Indiana had arrived to pick me up.

My experience with law enforcement up until this time had been nothing but negative, so I was expecting hard treatment. I had run from the police as a young teenager, and my relationship with the law had gone downhill from there. My heart was full of rebellion, and I was at a point where I didn't care anymore. Nothing much moved me. Still, it definitely surprised me when I saw that plainclothes detectives had come to get me. I had expected that Indiana would send a couple of uniformed officers, probably their toughest and sternest guys. But the sheriff from Boone County himself had come, along with another detective, and they were smiling at me. They were cordial, even, and to be honest with you, I was in shock.

I can imagine their thoughts about me when they saw my two black eyes and broken nose. But they kept on being nice. They put me in their car, where I met a third plainclothes detective. He was nice, too. For the first time in my life, I had a positive experience with law enforcement. The three of them asked me if I was comfortable and if there was anything they could get me. They asked if I was I hungry, and they stopped at McDonald's for some food.

I didn't know how to react to being treated like a human being. I was skeptical, to say the least. I kept waiting for them to pull the trigger, like they were softening me up for the kill. My thought was, *Are they just waiting to get me out of Florida's custody before they turn the screws on me, or what?*

As we began our drive back to Indiana, the sheriff explained to me how things stood. He said, "Mike, we have to talk about the charges that we have against you." Then they read me my rights, so I had the right to remain silent. The sheriff calmly explained the evidence they had against me. He said they had the car with our fingerprints in it. They had the eyewitness account of the gas station attendant, who had positively identified me. They had all the evidence against me except the weapon, because we had thrown that in the cornfield and they had failed to find it. I knew everything they told me was correct, and I knew they had a solid case. They then began to explain their system of felonies to me. There are type A, type B and type C felonies, with A being the highest or worst and C being the lowest.

After their explanations, to my utter amazement the sheriff addressed me seriously but with respect. To this day, I haven't figured out why he said it, but he said, "Mike, you know what? You're young. You get these charges put behind you, and you get on with your life."

I thought to myself, *What? Get on with my life? Are you kidding me? I'm going to do a bunch of time in your state, and then when you're done with me, I'm going to do a bunch more time in Michigan. What do you mean, get on with my life? Get past these charges? My life is OVER!*

I thought what he was saying was ludicrous, but he kept at it. He proceeded to tell me, "If you plead guilty, I will have all these charges reduced to a C felony, and you will face a maximum of 6 years."

I couldn't believe that at all. To prove it, he proceeded to get on the phone right there in the car, on the speaker. He called the prosecutor and told him, "I have the defendant here and this is what we discussed. . . I'm offering him this plea agreement. As prosecutor, do you agree?"

"Yes, I'll agree to that," a voice replied over the speaker.

Again, I was in shock. I still couldn't believe it. Before we had even left the State of Florida, they were offering me a plea agreement when they had me dead to rights. They could have given me life in prison there in Indiana, with all the charges against me and with my criminal history. Yet they were offering me a plea agreement for a maximum of 6 years! My head was reeling in confusion, but something deep in my heart said to go ahead and take the deal, so I agreed to it. I gave them verbal consent, and I began to confess to my crimes. I told them all the details and filled in all the blanks. I didn't leave anything out. I came clean with them, which was kind of a new experience for me around law enforcement. I guess the way they treated me had a positive effect on me.

We arrived at our destination, the Boone County Jail, which is directly across the street from that Shell gas station we had robbed. They moved me into a cell block, and right away I saw that this jail was different from any other jail I had been in. Nearly every jail is filled to capacity, and many are way over capacity. This one wasn't anywhere near full. It had a 240-person capacity, and at the time they only had 40 people incarcerated there. It was the quietest jail I've ever been to, and very peaceful compared to everywhere else I'd been.

Indiana was turning out to be a much better situation than I had any right to expect. I didn't realize at the time that I had the Lord to thank for some powerful intervention on my behalf. He had set His plan for me in motion, and I didn't even know it.

9

Born of the Spirit

Here I was, 24 years old, and I had already spent five years in prison. I had not even been out on parole for two years before I found myself facing the rest of my life behind bars. This time, I had been apprehended for armed robbery, kidnapping and auto theft in Indiana, a crime spree that had started with another armed robbery and auto theft in Michigan. I was at the lowest point of my life.

They moved me into my cell block, which held three or four other inmates. When they put me in my cell, I looked out my window and notice that I was directly across from the Shell gas station that I had robbed. Some coincidence.

Here I was, pacing my cell, thinking about my life and feeling so many emotions. Most of all, I was frustrated. I would never see my daughter again. Never be part of her life again. I thought I would never get married, never have a family. I'd never be free again. All the pain and hurt of my entire life culminated in this one moment of time—in this cell. It all came bubbling to the surface, all at once, and for the first time, I actually considered taking my own life.

The thought crossed my mind, *I should just end my life. End it all right here, right now, and be done with it.* The only thing that kept me from suicide was the thought of what it would do to my mom, my dad and my sisters. I knew it would absolutely devastate them. That was the one and only thing that kept me from following through on my suicidal thoughts.

In the midst of the worst time of my life, at the lowest point of my life, of all the things to remember, I remembered the words my friend Chris had spoken to me back during my first five years doing prison time. He was a fellow inmate who witnessed to me day after day while we lifted weights or played volleyball. I remember answering an altar call and going up front at a church service, at the Michigan Training Unit, where we met. Around that time, Chris had spoken the words he would say to me over and over again: "God *loves* you, Mike. He has a *plan* for your life."

I'll never forget that. Later in my cell, I took all my anger and frustration and I shook my fist up in the air toward God, and I said, "God if You love me so much, if You've got this great *plan* for my life, then how come my life is so messed up?"

Right then was the first time in my life that I heard the voice of God. It wasn't a booming voice from the corner of the cell. It wasn't Charlton Heston in a cloud. It was a still, small voice in my heart. If I had ever thought God would speak to me, I would have imagined that the first time, He would say something along the lines of, "Mike, you messed up. You've done too much. You've gone too far. You should have listened to Me when you had the chance."

He didn't say anything like that. He simply said, "Call on Me, Son. Call on Me."

Calling on God

Right there in that jail cell, I got on my hands and knees and began to cry for the first time in a long time. All the hardness of my heart had shut down my emotions so that I hardly ever expressed them. But I cried right then, and I did call on God. I raised my hands, and then I spread them out as I was kneeling there on the floor. I said, "God,

I've ruined this life. There's nothing I can do with it. I surrender it. I give it to You. Take it. You do whatever You want to with it, but my life belongs to You now."

With my Catholic upbringing, I began to confess my sins. I thought I had to confess all my sins, so I started way back. I said, "I'm sorry I pushed my sister down when I was four years old. . . I'm sorry I put the cat in the dryer when I was six . . ." Needless to say, I was there on the floor for quite a while.

When I got up off my knees, nothing had changed on the outside. I was still facing all those circumstances, still facing the prospect of spending the rest of my life in prison. But this time, something had changed on the *inside*—in my heart. When I looked into my heart, where I usually saw pain and anguish and frustration and anger, for the first time ever I found peace. A peace that I couldn't understand. A peace that wasn't based on the circumstances surrounding me. It made me get the biggest smile on my face. Suddenly, I understood why those guys Chris and Bible Jim were always smiling all the time.

I was born again! Born of the Spirit and alive to the Father! Later I would read about my experience in the Bible and I would find out that I had been recreated and made new. One of the Scriptures I read was John 3:1–4 (NKJV):

> There was a man of the Pharisees named Nicodemus, a ruler of the Jews. This man came to Jesus by night and said to Him, "Rabbi, we know that You are a teacher come from God; for no one can do these signs that You do unless God is with him."
>
> Jesus answered and said to him, "Most assuredly, I say to you, unless one is born again, he cannot see the kingdom of God."

> Nicodemus said to Him, "How can a man be born when he is old? Can he enter a second time into his mother's womb and be born?"

I realized that I had felt the same perplexity as Nicodemus when I heard Christians say they were born again. I didn't understand that Jesus was speaking about a spiritual experience. He went on to explain it to Nicodemus this way:

> That which is born of the flesh is flesh, and that which is born of the Spirit is spirit. Do not marvel that I said to you, "You must be born again." The wind blows where it wishes, and you hear the sound of it, but cannot tell where it comes from and where it goes. So is everyone who is born of the Spirit.
>
> John 3:6–8 NKJV

The "born-again" Christians I had wondered about knew it. They knew the key to life. Now I knew it, too.

I'll never forget the next morning. Volunteers would come into the jail to talk about God. They'd be let right into the cell block, and they'd come in with their Bibles in hand. Back in my previous incarceration experience, usually whenever the Bible volunteers would come in, everybody would see them with their Bibles under their arms and say, "Uh-oh, Bible thumpers. Time to go!" Then everyone would scatter.

Not on this morning! I walked up to this older gentleman, one of those volunteers who had walked in with a Bible in his hand, and I introduced myself.

"Hey, how you doing?" I said. "My name's Mike Benson."

"My name's John," he answered.

I explained to him what had happened the previous night, and he looked at me and said, "Son, you've been born again."

As I said, I had heard that expression before and it had bewildered me. So I just looked at him and said, "Well, I don't know what *born again* is, but it sure feels good!"

I began this relationship with John that lasted quite a while. He began to teach me about the Bible and tell me things about the Scriptures. I started spending my days immersed in the Word. We had cable TV available, and I'd get up in the morning and watch TBN (Trinity Broadcasting Network). I'd listen to these preachers on TV, and I'd never heard preaching like that before. They'd teach things about the Lord and about the Holy Spirit and about the anointing of the God. They'd teach about the call of God on your life and how God wants to bless you. I learned so much.

Wanting It All

One day, I remember hearing one of the TV preachers talk about the baptism in the Holy Spirit and speaking in tongues. This preacher was actually speaking in tongues right on TV. In my mind I was thinking, *What's this?* But in my spirit, I was drawn to it. Something inside me knew that it was true. I wanted that baptism!

Later on that day in my prayer time, in my alone time in my cell, I told the Lord, "God, I want it all. I want everything that Your Son died to give me. I've given You my life, and I want everything. I want to be baptized in the Holy Spirit."

I'll never forget staying up all night after that, reading my Bible and praying. I kept asking, "God, fill me with the Holy Spirit. God, fill me with the Holy Spirit." Then I'd stand there with my mouth open and my arms out, waiting for God to come put His Spirit on me and make me start speaking in tongues.

Finally, after three nights of doing that, I picked up my Bible in frustration and threw it down on the bunk, and I said, "I quit, God! I give up!"

"Good," God said. "I was waiting for you to give up. Now, are you ready to receive the baptism of the Holy Spirit?"

I stood there bewildered again. I had no idea what God meant. Here I was, trying to get it the whole time, but what I didn't understand about God and His Kingdom is that you don't try to get anything from Him. He has already given us everything we need. It is just like 2 Peter 1:3 (NLT) tells us: "By his divine power, God has given us everything we need for living a godly life. We have received all of this by coming to know him, the one who called us to himself by means of his marvelous glory and excellence."

I simply had to receive it by faith. "And whatever things you ask in prayer, believing, you will receive" (Matthew 21:22 NKJV). I'll never forget the moment I received. It was early morning. The sun was rising as I looked out the window, and I could see some fields out back. It was wintertime and there were no leaves on the trees, so the sun was coming up, shining through the branches. At just that moment, three deer came walking across a field right there out behind the jail. I could see their breath coming out as they walked. As the sun was shining through the trees and these deer were walking across the field, a rush of the Holy Spirit came inside my heart and *boom*, I started to speak in tongues.

As that language began to flow out of me, I could feel the power of God surging through my body. It felt like a big blanket, like a cloak was dropped on me. I began to rejoice in the power and presence of the Lord.

What I was experiencing was better than any drug I had ever done, any food I had ever eaten, any sexual experience I had ever had! I stood there in my cell laughing and weeping and praying in an unknown language. It was unknown to me, but not to God.

Later, I would come to know that when a person speaks in tongues, it is his or her spirit praying directly to God. First Corinthians 14:2 (NKJV) says, "For he who speaks in a tongue does not speak to men but to God, for no one understands him; however, in the spirit he speaks mysteries." And I would also find out that speaking in tongues would build me up: "He who speaks in a tongue edifies himself, but he who prophesies edifies the church" (1 Corinthians 14:4 NKJV).

I had a lot to learn, but now I was walking in the Holy Spirit, who would teach me all things. As Jesus told His disciples, "But the Helper, the Holy Spirit, whom the Father will send in My name, He will teach you all things, and bring to your remembrance all things that I said to you" (John 14:26 NKJV).

I had received the power of God not only in my life at salvation, but on my life as well through the anointing of the Holy Spirit—the very power I would walk in the rest of my days. A power greater than physical power or political power or financial power, and a power that is available to everyone who believes! Now Acts 1:8 would be true of me, too: "But you shall receive power when the Holy Spirit has come upon you; and you shall be witnesses to Me in Jerusalem, and in all Judea and Samaria, and to the end of the earth" (NKJV).

10

Living the Gospel

I became a role model prisoner at Boone County Jail. I really wasn't thinking that much about my court cases anymore. I was too overjoyed with being born again and receiving the baptism of the Holy Spirit. I started just feeding on the Word of God. I couldn't get enough of it. I ordered every spiritual growth book I could get my hands on—anything that taught me more about the things of the Spirit.

Of course, my mom wasn't too happy about it at first because she had raised me Catholic and I was straying off the reservation, so to speak. I remember I'd get into conversations with my sister Alicia on the phone, who was living the same type of partying lifestyle I had been. I would talk to her every day, and I'd tell her about things I read in Scripture and the discoveries and revelation I was getting. Slowly, over time, she ended up coming to know the Lord. I also focused on winning my cell mates. One by one, I slowly won them to the Lord, too.

When the jailer would open the cell block door and come in, he'd first get on his walkie-talkie and say, "Open A-Adam block," or "Open C-Charles block." I was in F block, and for that, the jailer would say, "Open F-Frank block." After the Spirit of God moved through that block and everybody in there was born again, the jailers themselves began to call it Faith block and say, "Open F-Faith block." The Lord was moving in a mighty way in that jail.

It was not long before the jailers were coming to the door of F block and asking me to come talk to them. They'd say, "Hey, we have this guy who came in last night on drunk driving. He's in a really bad spot. He doesn't have much family or anything. Can we put him in here with you guys?"

The jailers would actually come and ask permission to put a guy in with us when they figured maybe we could have a positive influence on him somehow. They'd send him into the cell, and we'd tell him, "Hey, anything you need, brother." Since we all put our commissary items together in a common box, if the new guy didn't have a toothbrush or deodorant or something, we'd give it to him. Then we'd hand him some food, some chips and some soups. We'd begin to love on him and witness the Lord Jesus to him. We began a ministry right there in the jail!

Even though I was born again, I was still hanging on to a lot of my old habits and old ways that hadn't yet been renewed in my mind. One of the things I had trouble with right away was my language. I had spent the last several years of my life swearing with every other word. I dropped the F-bomb almost every other word. We'd be playing cards and I'd lose a hand or something, and *bang*, I'd drop the F-bomb. Then my spirit would convict me.

Finally, I went to the Lord about it and said, "Lord, what am I going to do about my language?"

He instructed me that every time I swore, I'd have to stop what I was doing, go to my cell, get on my knees, and repent before Him. We'd be at the card table and I'd lose, and *bang*, I'd drop a swear word. Then I'd stop playing and say, "I'll be right back, guys." I'd go to my cell, get on my knees, and repent before the Lord. I don't know if it was the Lord working in me or if I just got tired of getting up and going to my cell and getting on my knees, but slowly, after a time, the swear words became less and less frequent.

A "Test of Faith" Fight

The first really major test of my faith came while I was in jail. They had just put this other guy, Randy Walker, in our jail cell, and he was different. Basically, he was a troublemaker. We witnessed to him over and over, but he wasn't having anything to do with it. It wasn't long before he and I got on each other's nerves.

In the mornings, I'd be watching TV, watching my favorite preachers. I had myself a little nest of Bibles right there, a stack of them, and I'd be all excited and taking notes as I watched the programs. Usually, everybody else would be sleeping. One morning, though, I was watching TV when Walker came out of his cell. He was slamming things around and flinging open his cell door so that it crashed into the wall, and he came out disgruntled and disheveled. Snarling at me, he said, "Hey, turn that blankety-blank stuff down!"

I looked over at him, and my flesh started rising up in me. My anger started coming up, but then I heard the still, small voice of the Lord say, "Turn it down." So I got up and turned the volume down.

Walker snarled again, "Yeah, that's what I thought. Yeah, you *better* turn it down." Then he went back to his cell.

I was irritated, but again I heard the Lord. He told me, "Turn it down some more."

"Come on, God," I remember saying to the Lord, "He needs to hear this stuff!" Still, I turned it down some more. Now the TV was so low that I was straining to hear it, and I was having trouble taking notes and following along in my Bible.

A couple minutes later, that cell door came swinging open again and Walker came out saying, "Man, I *told* you to turn that blankety-blankety-blank stuff down!"

Then I lost it. I had a fit of carnality. I got up. I kicked my shower shoes off. I touched the volume button. I turned it up as loud as it could go, and I told him, "*You* come over here and turn it down."

We proceeded to get into a fight. Of course, I won. I whipped him pretty good. I remember saying something stupid to him as he was lying on the ground with a bloody nose. Standing over him, I pointed down and said, "Don't ever mess with the Son of God again!"

Over the speakers, the jailers started yelling, "Lock down! Lock down!"

I went into my cell. After the adrenalin wore off, it hit me: *Oh, my gosh, I've just ruined my witness. Huh, some believer I am!* I told myself. *I was being a real good example for Jesus, wasn't I?*

The jailer came in, walked over to my cell, and said, "You all right?"

"Yeah, I'm fine," I told him.

"We watched everything on video," he said. "We heard everything that was going on. Don't worry—you're not going to be in any trouble because of this. No sanctions—you're not going to be locked down or anything. We know it was Randy. We're moving him out of this cell block."

That sounded good to me, not getting into any trouble over the fight. But I wasn't thinking about that kind of trouble. I was thinking about how I was supposed to be a believer in the Lord Jesus Christ. Here I was, His disciple, and I had just gotten into a fight with somebody! I was mortified because I still had this mindset that in order to be a Christian, you had to be perfect. You had to do everything just right. You couldn't mess up, couldn't do this, couldn't do that. I thought that way because that's the way I was raised.

I'll never forget how bad I felt. The whole thing really took me down for a while. Eventually, the feeling wore off and I got back into my Bible, back into studying the Word. The thing I love the most about God is His redemptive nature. He redeems everything. He redeemed this situation in a big way. It wasn't but a few weeks later that one of the jailers came to the door and said, "We have somebody in another cell block who really needs to talk to somebody."

I said, "Really? Who's that?"

"It's Randy Walker," he told me.

The very guy I just got into a fight with and beat up a couple weeks ago, I thought, *and now I'm supposed to witness to him after I did that to him . . .*

The jailer explained to me that Walker had just had a death in the family; a loved one he was close to had died. He was having a really hard time dealing with it, and he wanted to talk to me.

Whoa, I thought, *if he wants to talk to me, I better go see if I can help.*

I grabbed a bag of chips as a peace offering, and they walked me over to his cell block. They wouldn't let me go in because they weren't sure if he was trying a ploy to get his hands on me and take some revenge. They opened up the tray slot in the door that they slid the food trays through.

I got down, and there was Walker at the slot. He started telling me what had happened. His loved one had died, and he was feeling awful about it. He also said he was sorry for starting the fight with me. He said that even though he had been frustrated with me, he had also been watching me, and he could see that I was walking what I was talking. Pretty soon, tears started rolling down from his eyes.

"I want what you have," Walker told me.

I handed him a bag of chips through the door and said, "Brother, you need Jesus."

I grabbed his hand and led him in the sinner's prayer right there through the slot in the door. After I left that encounter, I felt ten feet tall and bulletproof. I felt like I was on top of the world. God had redeemed that situation. The word spread throughout the whole jail, and the Spirit of God started moving. Other inmates gave their lives to Christ, and it became one of the greatest experiences.

A "Crazy" Call

I went to court in Indiana, and the plea agreement I entered was taken before the judge for consideration. The judge accepted it. I was instructed to order my plea officially for the record, so I pled guilty to robbery and auto theft. The judge sentenced me to six years.

Part of my plea agreement was that there would be no modification of my sentence. In Indiana, once you got a certain prison sentence, after you served half of that time (so in my case, three of the six years), you could file a petition with the court to have a modification made. They could grant a modification because of good behavior or due to other circumstances, and you could end up not doing the rest of your time. Basically, you could do only half your time and then be done. But one of the stipulations the prosecutor made in my case was that there would be no modification of my sentence, so I was sentenced to six full years in the Indiana Department of Corrections.

Not long after my court date, I was sent to the reception and diagnostic center in Plainfield, Indiana. From there they sent me to Westville Correctional Facility, which was notorious in the northern section of Indiana. Westville is an extremely violent prison that houses a lot of young inmates. I was placed on the educational side.

Just before I left jail for prison, Tim, a guy who came in with several other volunteers every Wednesday to do Bible studies with us, had a little talk with me. He had become a mentor to me in my Christian walk, and on this particular day he came into my cell and sat down with something on his mind. I made him a cup of instant coffee and we were sitting there talking, and then he let it out.

"Brother Mike," he said, "I believe the Lord has called you to preach the Gospel."

Outwardly, I smiled at Tim and said, "Oh yeah? Amen, brother, amen."

Inwardly, I thought, *Is he crazy? Did he fall on something and bump his head?*

I could understand that God had saved me. I could understand that He had forgiven me of my sins. I could understand all of that, but what I could not understand was why God would use somebody like me to represent Him. It seemed like a crazy call. Here I was a prisoner with seven felony offences. How would God use somebody like me to represent Him?

When Tim made that comment to me, I could not believe it, I could not receive it, and I definitely could not understand it. There was that aspect of it seeming to me like a crazy call, and then there was the aspect of my stereotype about preachers or pastors. I had this idea in my head about what it took to be a man of God, and I certainly didn't fit the stereotype. I didn't even come close—not even in the same ballpark. And I had my Catholic stereotype of a priest in robes, who sat around and prayed all day. Plus, he was never allowed to get married, so that definitely was not an option for me. Then there was the "protestant" stereotype in my head of a preacher in a checkered suit, who drove a beat-up car and married a plain-Jane-looking wife. (She never wore makeup, but always wore a dress down to her ankles.) For some reason, those religious stereotypes were stuck in my brain.

It wasn't until I was at Westville prison that God broke those stereotypes and opened me up to the idea of accepting my calling to preach His Gospel. They were holding services at Westville, and similar to the Michigan Department of Corrections, in Indiana you had to have a C for Catholic or a P for Protestant or an M for Muslim on your ID to attend one. I got a P and went to the Protestant services. One of the brothers who also attended came up to me one time and said, "Man, you got to see this guy; you got to hear this guy who is coming up. Man, this guy is awesome! He's on fire!"

"Cool, man," I responded, not really knowing what to expect. I walked into the service and there was a young guy there, probably in his early forties. He looked really cool. He was dressed in a contemporary suit; no checkered suit for him! When he got up behind the podium and opened his mouth to preach the Word of God, the power of God came out of that man in such a way that I was totally blown away. Right there in that service, my stereotype of preachers was broken—shattered, as a matter of fact.

I remember thinking to myself, *If that's what a preacher of the Gospel is and that's what You've called me to be, God, count me in. I'm in, Lord, I'm in!*

I went up to the guy afterward and began to talk to him. He shared some of his testimony with me. Although he had never been to prison or jail, he was one of the South's largest drug kingpins back in his day. He wore a Mohawk and had tattoos everywhere. He showed me a picture of his wife, and man, she was really good looking. He told me their story. He had met his wife in a strip club when she was a stripper, and they had gotten married. Then a preacher had come to them one day when they were at the end of a several-day drug and alcohol binge. Their souls were dried out, and they were empty and lost and dead inside. This preacher ministered the Word of life to them, and they were born again. Now they had a church and an organization from which people traveled all over the world preaching the Gospel of Jesus Christ.

When I heard this man's testimony of how God had redeemed his life from drugs, crime, emptiness, and death to a life of ministering to other people, I was able through faith to receive my call to preach the Gospel. After I received it, I started to discover that God had gifted me for it. I would hold Bible studies in our dorm at Westville. Several brothers would come in and open up the Scriptures, and God would give me revelation. We'd be praying for people, praying for the sick, and they'd get healed. We'd lay hands on people, and they'd get baptized with the Holy Spirit.

God's Spirit began to move in and through me in a mighty way. I was doing ministry before I even knew that it was called ministry. God was ministering to others through me. I believe that's what a real minister is. It's not somebody who has a job or a title, or somebody who has a position of authority. A minister is a servant, a vessel of the Lord Jesus Christ. A minister becomes the hands and feet of Jesus Christ in the earth. A minister is a tangible representation of the Lord Jesus Christ to people everywhere.

As the Lord began to move through me and speak through me, He would confirm His Word through signs and wonders. And I wasn't thinking anymore about where I was. I wasn't thinking about whether I was in prison or whether I had my freedom. My freedom didn't come the day the government released me from prison. My freedom came the day I let Jesus Christ into my heart. That's when my freedom came. Freedom comes from the inside out, and I was living in total freedom even though I was incarcerated.

11

Testing Time

It was an ordinary day. There was nothing spectacular about it. I was on a picnic table in one of the day rooms at Westville prison, reading my Bible, as was my custom most days. Suddenly, I felt a prompting from the Holy Spirit, and the Lord spoke to me. He said, "Write your judge a letter asking him to modify your sentence."

Two things were wrong here in my estimation. Number one, part of my plea agreement was that I would not be eligible for any modification of sentence, and the judge had agreed with that. That meant I would have to do the whole six years. Number two, I had only been in the Indiana Department of Corrections, including my stay at the Boone County Jail, for about two years. In order to even qualify or be able to petition the court for a modification, I'd need to have served at least three of those years.

Yet I had learned a lot of things, chief among them that I was living a life of faith. I was now living by the laws of the unseen realm, the spiritual realm. And God's ways are higher than man's ways in any realm; His thoughts are higher than our thoughts. I had started to learn how to live in the miraculous and how to live according to God's plans. So even though my head was thinking contrary to what I had heard from God, my heart was telling me to do it.

I wrote the letter. I sat down and handwrote it on a legal pad. Once I got the rough draft ready, I planned to have it typed up in legal format to make it look presentable. In fact, I was heading down to the law clerk at the prison to get that done when the Holy Spirit told me, "Don't have it typed! Send it just like it is."

Whenever you file anything in court, they are very particular about how it is worded and how it is written. Everything has to be just right. But I trusted what the Lord told me, and I put my letter in an envelope and sent it in the mail in my own handwriting, just the way it was.

About a month after that, I was called to appear on a writ. A writ is when you're in custody in one jurisdiction (as I was, in Indiana) and you have pending charges in another jurisdiction (as I had, in Michigan). They want to take care of your case while it's fresh, so to speak, so they'll send for a writ. (They file a writ to get custody of you.) It's part of the interstate agreement on detainers. Basically, one jurisdiction borrows a prisoner from another jurisdiction to take care of a court case that the prisoner has pending in that jurisdiction. Michigan was calling Indiana, wanting to come get me because they had some charges they wanted to take care of with me.

Because of the writ, I was picked up and taken to Michigan to face the original charge that all this time I was serving stemmed from. They brought me to the Kent County Jail to face the original car theft charge from when Jeff and I had stolen that car.

A lot of changes in the law had come about in this time. It was a good thing for me that the O'Hare Law had been repealed, which was an attempt by the Michigan Legislature to get tough on crime. If you were sentenced to 4 to 20 years, like I was, and you were paroled and committed another felony while out on parole, you would have to finish the remainder of your original sentence—the "tail" end of it—and then start serving the next sentence after that. In my case, I would have had to serve the rest of my 20 years before serving time for the charge of car theft. But that law was only on the books for a year because it was having an unforeseen effect. Michigan discovered that the law was taking small-time felons and turning them into fugitives. If a guy stole a car and he had a 20-year tail, there was no way he was coming in willingly to finish that and then serve another sentence. He'd become a dangerous fugitive instead.

Thankfully for me, that law was repealed, so here I was in the county jail with a court-appointed attorney checking out my options. He was telling me that the best he could do for me was probably a year of jail time if I pled guilty to a felonious auto theft. I had prayed prior to going to Michigan, because by this time I had learned that I was under orders. My life didn't belong to me anymore; my life belonged to the Lord Jesus Christ. I didn't do things according to my own understanding or my own wishes or desires anymore. I was now a son of the King, and I was His to command. I prayed and asked Him about these cases in Michigan, and the word I got from the Lord was, "No felony." I knew that I would not settle for anything other than a misdemeanor in Kent County.

The interstate agreement on detainers states that once another jurisdiction came and got me from Indiana, they had 180 days in which to settle all the charges they had pending against me. If Michigan came and got me and didn't take care of things by the end of 180 days, whatever charges were held against me in that state would be dropped automatically. After I had spent four months in the Kent County Jail, I started getting excited. I knew I still had a big case pending against me in Belding, where Jeff and I had robbed the bar, had tied up the barmaid, and had taken her car. I knew a case of that magnitude wouldn't be settled in a month or two; these things take a long time.

Here I had been four months in the jail already with that little charge of car theft against me, and my court-appointed lawyer was getting very frustrated with me. He would come to me with a plea bargain again and again, and I'd say, "No, no, I'll take a misdemeanor."

He'd go back and forth with the prosecutor and come back and tell me, "Look, you know this is the best I can do for you. You plead guilty to a felony, and you get six months. Six months—that's all! And considering your record and your history and all the charges against you, that's a *really* good deal. Just take the plea agreement."

"No," I said again. "We can go to trial on it because I think it was a misdemeanor."

I'll never forget what that lawyer told me on his last visit to me. He said that just as he was leaving his office to see me one final time, he got a letter stating that the prosecutor had agreed to drop my charge to a misdemeanor and a plea agreement with time served. I went in front of a judge, who sentenced me to time served on a high-court misdemeanor, the most serious level of misdemeanor in Michigan, but not the same as having another felony on my record. Praise the Lord!

I was feeling pretty good because I was doing the math in my head. I had served five months at the Kent County Jail, and I knew that either a) I'd be picked up and brought back to Indiana, or b) another jurisdiction would come and get me to try to deal with the charges against me, and there was a very good likelihood that the charges would be dropped. Not too long after that, I was told that officials from Ionia County had come to get me. The City of Belding was in Ionia County, which is where Jeff and I had committed that armed robbery, tying up the barmaid and taking her car.

They took me to the Ionia County Jail. A lot had changed in my two years of being incarcerated. Having given my life to the Lord, I no longer went to the law library to study the laws and try to find loopholes for a way out of my charges. Now when I got somewhere, I went right to work on the people in the jail cells, witnessing to them. When we were escorted out onto the recreation yard, a little square concrete enclosure in the jails, I'd be right up there talking to the officers, witnessing about Jesus and telling them about what God had done in my life. Wherever I went, I was on a mission to win souls, and I was keeping a score of how many people I was winning to the Lord Jesus Christ.

Letting Go of a Loophole

They appointed me one of the best lawyers in town. I figured it was because they were going to send me up the river for a long time, and they wanted to make sure they had their bases covered. If they could show there was good representation on my behalf, I wouldn't come back on an appeal or something and claim that I had gotten ineffective assistance with counsel. This lawyer sat down for an interview with me and started going over everything.

I told him, "Hey, man, you know the 180-day agreement on detainers. That's going to be up, and there's no way they can do this in time."

"I brought that up with the prosecutor," he told me, "and the prosecutor said that they don't have a detainer on you now. There's no longer a warrant out for your arrest since you've been incarcerated in Indiana, but you can still press the 180-day rule if you choose to do so."

A detainer is like a warrant. Once I was arrested and put in custody in Indiana, they took the warrant out of the system for me. But if I chose to press the detainer rule, they would send me back to Indiana, wait until I was done there, and then deal with me after that.

"They'll be a lot less likely to be in a bargaining mood if you insist on the 180-day rule," my lawyer told me. "It would be better just to take care of the charges now since you're already in Michigan. Don't make them come get you a second time."

"Okay," I said. "I can understand that."

I started praying to the Lord, asking Him what to do about this situation. I didn't hear anything from Him, though. He wasn't giving me any specific instructions; He wasn't telling me anything to do. So I just trusted and kept praying and reading Scripture, and before long my lawyer came to me and said that they had offered me a very good deal. They said they would offer me a plea agreement where I would face 15 years for the robbery, kidnapping and car theft.

In legal terms, that was a very good plea agreement considering my record and considering I had been on parole. That was a very, very good plea agreement. I think Michigan just wanted to save money by avoiding a trial because anybody in their right mind would have taken 15 years. But something inside me was not comfortable with 15 years.

At another court hearing after that, my lawyer and I were talking while we waited, and he said, "Hang on a second, I'll be back in a minute," and he left. They put me in a holding cell, and three hours later my lawyer came back in. I was just a little bit upset.

He said, "Come with me," and they took me out of the holding cell and brought me to this room, like an interview room, and sat me down. My lawyer had a huge smile on his face, and he had a folder in his hand. He began to explain to me, "Mike, as we were sitting there talking, something about this 15 years didn't sit right with me."

I thought, *Wow, that makes two of us.*

"So I went into the law library," he continued, "because I wanted to do some research. I just felt compelled to go in there."

Hmm, you felt compelled, huh? I was thinking. I didn't know if he was a believer or not, but watching his demeanor and hearing his language, I pretty much assumed he was not. When he said he felt compelled though, I thought, *There's my God at work in this!*

The lawyer said he was looking through some law books, and he said he didn't know why, but he hopped on the computer and checked the National Crime Information Center (NCIC), which is a nationwide database that keeps track of warrants that are out for peoples' arrest. Every state registers outstanding warrants with the NCIC. Then, if a police officer in Michigan unknowingly pulls someone over who is wanted in Arizona, when the officer runs the person's name and information, the warrant in Arizona will show up via the NCIC. My lawyer hopped onto the NCIC database and found me a loophole.

"The Belding Police Department still has the warrant out for your arrest from almost three years ago," he told me. "It's still on the NCIC—which means you fall into the 180-day time for the interstate agreement on detainers—which means you can have all these charges dropped immediately!"

I was about to come out of my seat, thinking, *Yes! Yes! My God—that's my God at work!*

And then I heard this voice on the inside say, "Plead guilty."

And I said, "Get thee behind me, Satan!"

But when you get know somebody, you get to know that person's voice. And I knew the Voice that was speaking to me, even if I didn't like what I was hearing. A lot of people say they know God, when what they really mean is that they know *about* God. There's a big difference. To become really intimate with someone, you have to spend time communicating. Too much of our prayer involves one-way communication where we spend time praying and putting in requests with God. But that's not the same as two-way communication where we listen to what *He* has to say to us. By this time in my walk with God, I had gotten to know God's voice. I had a relationship with Him, and I knew I needed to listen to Him.

More than anything on the face of the planet, God desires to have a relationship with His children. His ultimate desire is to pour out His love, His affection and all of His blessings out on His children. Yes, it's true that He sent His Son, Jesus Christ, to die on the cross for our sins in the greatest act of love ever. But He did that because sin became an obstacle that had to be dealt with after mankind's Fall in the Garden of Eden. God's real heart and purpose for creating the human race in the first place was *relationship with Him*. His desire for intimacy with us did not change once Adam and Eve ate the forbidden fruit; it just took a Savior after that to restore that relationship to what God originally intended it to be.

God our Father wants each of us to come home to Him through the saving power of His Son, Jesus Christ. He doesn't want us following a list of rules or checking off things that we should or should not do. He wants us spending time with Him in relationship, getting to know His voice, and following Him. Above everything else, He wants relationship with you and me.

I had entered into that kind of relationship with my heavenly Father, and even though everything in my head told me I was crazy to plead guilty, in my heart I knew it was the Father telling me that was what He wanted me to do. What a test! This was another major crossroad in my life. It was a pivotal moment. Would I choose to obey my Lord, or would I go with my own understanding? Clearly, I had a way out. I had my loophole, yet God was telling me not to use it.

Even though there was a battle going on in my mind, in an instant I decided to put all that aside and follow the Lord. I proceeded to tell my lawyer that I was going to plead guilty, and then I proceeded to tell him why I was pleading guilty. Right away, I found out that he definitely was *not* saved. He completely came unglued on me. He thought I was out of my mind, but I was determined to follow what I had heard from God. Needless to say, our conversation did not end well.

Finally, my day in court arrived. I remember that day clearly. Prisoners were held in a holding room or cell adjacent to the courtroom, and on this particular day there were a lot of us. The courtroom itself was also packed. A lot of cases were being heard, and one by one the prisoners would be let out to enter the courtroom and appear before the judge. All we would see from the holding cell was someone going out a door, and then a half hour to an hour later, the prisoner would come back in holding a piece of paper.

All the other prisoners in the cell would be asking, "What'd you get? What'd you get?"

On this particular day in court, each time a prisoner would leave, he'd come back with a sullen look on his face and say, "I got eighteen months," or "I got two years."

We were amazed because most of these guys were first-time offenders. They were in trouble with the law for the very first time, so you'd think that in most cases they'd get probation or community service. Relatively speaking, they had committed petty crimes like stealing property or fleeing or looting or something like that. It became painfully obvious that this judge was not playing any games. These first-time offenders were coming back with heavy sentences, and I felt as if they all had a look on their face like they were watching me and thinking, *We'll feel better once he goes because he's the one who has the most charges and the worst criminal record. He'll be facing the most time!* It was as if they couldn't wait to see what this harsh judge would do to me.

I walked out into the courtroom, and the judge asked me and my attorney to step up to the bench. We stepped up, and my lawyer started off by explaining to the judge that he had advised his client (me) to take the plea agreement. He explained how the state had messed up because the police officer had left the warrant for his client's arrest on the NCIC. That constituted a detainer, which, according to the 180-day detainer law, meant the client could beat the charges on a technicality.

"But," my lawyer told the judge, "it is my client's decision to plead guilty anyway. *Why*, I do not know, but this is totally at my client's discretion, and this is totally my client's decision."

My lawyer was making his case for his counsel on public record so that no one could blame him or come back later and say he hadn't represented me very well.

The prosecutor got up and explained that the police department had indeed made a mistake. Then she started talking about my crimes and how I was on parole when I committed the charges under consideration. She also explained that I was currently on loan from Indiana because I was serving time for a similar crime. Her gist was that obviously, I was a heinous criminal and that the judge should throw the book at me.

After my lawyer and the prosecutor were done, the judge looked up from his papers and looked right at me.

"I want to hear from him," he told them. "Young man," he said to me, "you've clearly got these charges beat, yet you're pleading guilty. Why is that?"

I looked up at him and said, "Your Honor, I don't know where you're at spiritually, but with all respect, it really doesn't matter to me. If you look at the file in front of you, the man who committed all those crimes is a dead man. I'm a new creature in Christ Jesus. I know that doesn't erase what I did in the past, but what it does is give me the courage to stand here and take responsibility for what I have done."

Right there in open court, I began to share my testimony about what the Lord Jesus had done in my heart. After I was finished, the judge began to file through his papers for a few minutes.

Suddenly, he picked up his gavel and said, "I hereby sentence you to six months in the county jail, with credit for time served. Have a nice life, Mr. Benson."

Bam, he slammed the gavel down. A big gasp went through the courtroom. People could not believe what they had just witnessed—I had just pled *guilty* and the judge had given me six months in jail, with credit for time served. And I was no first-time offender like the people who had appeared before me and had gotten eighteen months to two years for first-time felony offenses. I had pled guilty to armed robbery, kidnapping, and car theft, no less, and those were by no means my first or only crimes. Yet the judge saw something—or rather, he saw Someone—in me that made all the difference.

I have to say, I was feeling a little bit excited. I came walking back into the holding cell and I had my orange jumpsuit on, with my hands shackled at my side, with my accessories on (handcuffs and belly chains), and I had my papers. I must admit, I did walk in gloating a little bit.

They all asked what I got, and I shook the paper and said, "Six months."

Everybody in the holding cell sat back with their jaws dropping. When I left court and got back to my jail cell, I shared with the guys what had happened. Two of the guys in the jail had been really resistant to the Gospel, but hearing my testimony of what happened in court pushed them over the edge, and they finally gave their lives to the Lord.

Having been charged with armed robbery, kidnapping, and car theft and receiving a sentence of six months in the country jail, with credit for time served, was a miracle in itself. I was seeing the hand of God in my life at work, ordering my steps so I could fulfill His plan for my future. Up until I gave my life to the Lord, the enemy, Satan, had a plan for my future, and I was a participant in his plan. That plan was to steal, kill, and destroy my life, my soul and everyone around me that he could reach. The moment I chose life over death—the moment I chose the Author of life and His will for my life, I got on a totally different path. As Jesus said in John 10:10, "The thief does not come except to steal, and to kill, and to destroy. I have come that they may have life, and that they may have it more abundantly."

I'll never forget the moment when the police officers came to pick me up and transport me from Ionia back to Indiana. I got in the back of the car, and then they looked over my papers. One officer said to the other, "Is this right? It can't be! We better go and check to make sure."

One officer got out of the car and went back in to check. The other officer started questioning me: "Did you get six months jail time, with credit for time served, for all these charges?"

I just sat in the back and smiled.

He said, "Man, you must have had a good attorney."

I said, "Yep, I had the best Attorney anybody could have." And I wasn't talking about my earthly representation; I was talking about my Advocate with the Father, Jesus Christ.

The officers finally got it squared away. As I left Ionia, I felt such joy and jubilation. I had won several people to the Lord Jesus Christ while I had been there. I had witnessed to two officers at the jail and won them to Jesus. I had walked out of that courtroom victorious and shared my testimony. Thinking back on all that, it was a good day!

I still had to finish up my six years in Indiana, of course, and after that, I had to face my parole violation. I could get several years for that, too. I wasn't quite out of the woods, but God wasn't done with me yet. God had me in a process of preparation. In a process of preparation, a lot of pruning has to happen and a lot of things have to be learned so a person can live by faith. I was learning how to trust God in everything, in every situation. Obeying the Lord about pleading guilty and seeing the amazing, unexpected result taught me a lot about the importance of following God's lead.

Motion Denied!

Returning to Indiana, it wasn't even two days before I got called up front to pick up legal mail. It was a letter from the court in Boone County. In my mind I thought, *Oh man, here we go.* I had forgotten all about that letter I had written asking them to modify my sentence. As I opened up the letter and read it, I have to admit, I was astonished. The court had granted my modification hearing and had set a date. It was two months away, which meant I'd be going back to Boone County Jail soon.

An officer came to pick me up for the two-hour drive back down to Lebanon, Indiana. When I got to the jail, some of my former jailers were still there. They told me I had court first thing in the morning. The next morning, I went to the court and it was just me. I didn't even have a lawyer. It was me and an officer. I found that the court had received my letter and had looked at it. Even though it wasn't in the proper legal format prescribed by the court, it was still considered a legal motion. I had handwritten it and had also signed my name to it. They looked at the motion and found out what case it involved, and they sent the motion on to the prosecutor.

The prosecutor then had a certain amount of time to answer the motion. He could have answered it by saying to the judge, "I request that you deny this motion based on the plea agreement, based on this, based on that . . ." Then that would have been the end of my motion. But probably because it was a handwritten letter, it sat on the prosecutor's pile, and when he glanced at it, he probably figured it was a letter from a prisoner trying to present a motion. He totally ignored it. He never did answer the letter.

The court had made a copy of it, though, and in the prescribed time, according to the procedures of the court, they granted me a hearing because there was no rebuttal from the prosecutor. The motion was therefore automatically granted. I don't think the prosecutor meant for that to happen; he just neglected my handwritten letter rather than bothering with it, and they granted me a hearing based on no rebuttal. Again, God's hand was at work.

We got into court and the judge came in and asked the prosecutor to open up. The prosecutor started by saying, "This defendant already got an awesome plea agreement. Part of that plea agreement was no modification of sentence. So his motion should not have been granted by this court . . ."

He went on and on, and then the judge asked him, "Well, how come you had all kinds of time to answer this motion, and you never answered it? What's going on?"

The prosecutor made some excuse for ignoring my motion, and then the judge said to me, "What do you have to say in your defense, young man?"

I got up and did the same thing that I did in Ionia. I testified about how I was saved in the very jail that sat across the street from the very gas station I had previously robbed about three years ago. I explained how the Lord has been working in my life. I mentioned that at Westville Correctional Facility, one day I had been studying my Bible on a picnic table when the Lord had spoken to me and told me to write this letter about a motion. "And here I stand before you," I finished.

This judge looked at me and said, "I could be totally off, Mr. Benson, but something tells me that if I let you out of this court, I'd never have to worry about you getting in trouble again. Is that correct?"

I said, "Your Honor, that's correct."

He said, "But because of the plea agreement and the nature of it, I cannot modify your sentence, Mr. Benson."

"Okay," I said.

He said, "What I can do is resentence you. So I hereby resentence you to time served on a 3-year sentence. Case closed."

Just like that, I was done serving time in Indiana. The judge had both denied my motion for modification and in the same breath resentenced me to time served. Again, it was another unbelievable victory the Lord granted me. I would not be returning to prison, at least not in Indiana. My time of incarceration there was over. I was then returned to the Boone County Jail. The jail was instructed to notify the authorities in Michigan that if the Michigan Department of Corrections did not come get me within a certain amount of time, I would be released.

Missing It

This was another crucial time in my life. Everybody misses it sometimes, misses hearing from God or misses understanding how He is working. In life's learning process, some of the greatest learning opportunities come when we make mistakes, when we miss it.

This was one of those times for me. Instead of consulting the Lord and asking Him what was next after my resentencing, I chose to lean on my own understanding. I figured that because I had beaten all these hardcore, heavy charges hanging over my head, which I could have received life in prison for, that meant I had beaten everything.

I firmly believed that I would be freed in Indiana and that I wouldn't have to return to jail in Michigan.

Surely after all that, a parole violation is nothing for God to handle, I thought. *Surely He will deliver me from that, too. Man, the officers from Michigan probably won't even come get me. They're probably going to let me go. I'll soon be as free on the outside as God has made me on the inside!*

I only had that parole violation left back in Michigan, and the Lord had already delivered me from far more serious charges. I wound up doing just under three years of time for all those other charges. It didn't make any sense to me to think that I had come this far toward freedom, but that I wouldn't make it the rest of the way. I knew that God could make it happen and that He would make it happen, but I was working on my own timetable. The factor I left out was God's timing. That's where I missed it.

12

The Call of God

My heart and mind were set on freedom, and I figured my freedom was coming soon. I had yet to learn that it was coming soon, all right, but it wasn't going to be in my time. It was going to be in God's time. My times were in the hands of the Lord. I hadn't missed it on the substance of His promises—I would see freedom. But as I said in the previous chapter, I had missed it on the timing. To my utter dismay, a little less than a month later, officers from the Michigan Department of Corrections arrived at the jail in Indiana to pick me up and return me to prison in Michigan.

I was transported directly to Jackson State Prison to go through a violation hearing in front of a parole board member. When I arrived, I was placed in the reception and guidance center (RGC). The next day, I had a hearing in front of a parole board member, who basically read my parole violation and added, "By the way, you've committed several other felonies after the fact."

Hearing him put it that way, I thought to myself, *Hey, I'll do what worked in the other two cases—I'll just share my testimony.* I began to share my salvation story with this gentleman, and he stood there and looked at me through his glasses, unimpressed. He showed absolutely no emotion, no expression on his face.

After I finished, he asked me, "Are you done?"

"Yes," I answered."

"All right," he said, and *bang*, he sentenced me to 24 months for a parole violation. It was what we call a "flop." Just like that, he gave me two years in prison for violating my parole.

All those charges behind me and all that time served, and now I had been sentenced to almost the same amount of time for a parole violation as for everything else together. I couldn't understand it, couldn't comprehend it. God knew what He was doing, but I sure didn't know. I had no idea. In time, it would become clear, which was another lesson I was about to learn.

Operation Starting Line

In Jackson, Prison Fellowship's Operation Starting Line (OSL) came in to minister. Prison Fellowship is the ministry founded by Chuck Colson, who was a former lawyer for the Nixon Administration. As part of the Watergate scandal, Chuck Colson was one of several people who went to prison. While in a federal prison he was born again, and he wrote a book about it called *Born Again* (Bantam, 1977; Chosen, 2008). It was actually the first book I ever read as a Christian.

Chuck Colson started Prison Fellowship (PF) to reach prisoners with the Gospel of Jesus Christ. He also started PF as an advocacy ministry that would be politically involved. With Chuck Colson's notoriety and his influence in political circles, PF soon grew into a worldwide ministry. Back in 2001, PF started Operation Starting Line, which was an evangelistic blitz where they would go into a state and try to visit every single prison there with an evangelistic program. They would bring in platform artists, musicians, people doing feats of strength, and ex-offenders giving their testimonies. All of it was geared toward evangelism and winning souls for Christ.

I'll never forget when Operation Starting Line came into Jackson. By that time in my walk with Christ, I knew I was called to preach the Gospel. I knew God had gifted me with His Spirit and given me a prophetic anointing. I was wrestling with the whole question of how God was going to get me plugged into a church when I got out. I was also wondering how I would be used when I got out. I still had a little of the prisoner mentality in my thinking, so these questions seemed huge to me. But OSL brought in a man named Rocco Morelli. He was one of the OSL platform artists, and he came to give his testimony about how he was in the La Cosa Nostra Mafia, the American branch of the Sicilian Mafia. He was very highly connected in the Philadelphia Mafia, or the infamous Pizza Connections, which made headlines due to the many pizza shops that were used as a cover for illegal activities. He gave his testimony about how he was sentenced to 50 years for his Mafia connections, and how the Lord miraculously delivered him from 50 years in prison. Now he was travelling and sharing his testimony all over the country. He was also writing a book called *Forgetta 'bout It: From Mafia to Ministry* (Bridge-Logos, 2007) and doing all these other things for the Lord. It was during his testimony at Jackson that the realization or the revelation that God would use me in the same way sank into my spirit. All my doubt was washed away by Morelli's powerful testimony.

Jackson was also the place where I preached a sermon for the first time ever. A guy named Jerry and a few other inmates were in charge of Bible studies there. Every second Sunday of the month in the auditorium, instead of having regular service with a guest speaker coming in, we would be divided up into different sections, basically along denominational lines. Each section had a teacher or leader, and Jerry was the leader of the Spirit-filled section. Fifty of us were in that group. Jerry gave powerfully anointed sermons, but he was going to be transferred soon to another facility. He wanted me to take his place, and I agreed to do it. My first message was on the power of the anointing. I gave an altar call, and twelve out of the fifty guys made decisions for Jesus. It was quite an experience. That was the first time I ever preached a sermon.

Now Praying at the I-Max . . .

I spent about eighteen months in Jackson Prison before I was transferred to Ionia Maximum Correctional Facility, or I-Max. It is where the worst, most violent prisoners are housed in level 5 security. It's the most secure prison in Michigan. There was a level 2 section, though, which consisted of two pole barns set up as a dormitory setting with six-man open cubicles. The level 2 prisoners were basically the work force for the level 5 sections. They worked in the kitchen, did the housekeeping, and cleaned in the level 5 facility. I was transferred into this part of I-Max. In the prisoners' minds, level 2 I-Max is considered a very prestigious place to go because it houses only a small population, about four hundred inmates, compared to the thousands in other prisons. It is also a nice, clean facility, and for me it was close to home.

As soon as I got to I-Max, of course I got plugged in with the local Body of Christ. I signed up to attend services, and I remember going to them and thinking they were a bit dead. I-Max services were unique because they were videotaped and fed via closed-circuit cameras to the level 5 prisoners, who have a constitutional right to worship services. Those guys needed Christ, so I felt it was really important that the services reach them and minister to them. I quickly found favor with a chaplain in I-Max's church, and I started putting some pressure on him to change the way services were done, specifically in regard to the volunteers who were brought in. The volunteers were great guys, but sometimes their focus seemed off. One of the volunteers who did Sunday services had a great heart and a desire to share with the prisoners, but he didn't seem to feel a calling to impart any type of revelation. He basically spent all his time talking either about himself or his family member who was terminally ill. I felt bad for him, but even worse for the prisoners who had to listen to his repetitive personal stories when what they should have been hearing was the good news of the Gospel.

The situation with the I-Max services grieved my spirit tremendously because church is meant to be a place where we experience the living God. It is also supposed to be a place where we fellowship with each other and give our worship to God, not watch performers on a platform. And like the Temple in the Bible, it's a place of giving where we can contribute our finances to support the Kingdom. People went to the Temple in Jerusalem to offer sacrifices, to offer worship, to offer praise to the living God, and to experience His presence. Much of that was lacking in the I-Max services.

There's something powerful that happens in the dynamic of believers coming together in agreement, with an open hunger and thirst for the presence of God. In services like that, His presence fills and satisfies areas of our hearts that no message or sermon could ever touch. After experiencing services like that, it's hard to settle for lifelessness. It's also great to go to a service and hear a message full of really good, anointed preaching and teaching. Those messages are edifying, and they uplift you, give you strength, and impart grace and life to the hearers. But after hearing messages like that, then when you hear a message that isn't good, much less anointed, it's a letdown instead of being uplifting.

Listening time after time to this brother telling us about his relative's medical condition eventually became torturous to me. Some of the older believers who had been there for a while were used to him, though. They thought this volunteer was great, and he did have his strong points. Yet people can get used to the status quo and usually don't like change, even when change is needed. Some people really wanted this guy to stay, but I felt he wasn't making the most of the opportunity to present the Gospel to those who needed it so badly. My persistence about having a new volunteer come in was met with quite a bit of resistance in the local Body of Christ, but I kept at it. You might even say I caused the first "church fight" at I-Max. I admit that maybe I didn't handle things as well as I could have. I was struggling for balance—or at least tactfulness—at this time in my life because I felt so strongly in my spirit about certain things. And anything I felt strongly about, I would pursue so passionately that it would always cause conflict or trouble. That was exactly the situation with my sense about the I-Max services and with my persistence about bringing changes.

One day I went to God in my private prayer time and asked Him about it: "Lord, what's going on here? What's up? Am I supposed to be timid and back down? Should I be lowly and meek about this? Or am I supposed to stand up? Am I coming on too strong? What's going on?"

That was when the Lord reminded me of His calling on my life. He called me out of Ezekiel chapter 3, in which He tells the prophet Ezekiel,

> Behold, I have made your face strong against their faces, and your forehead strong against their foreheads. Like adamant stone, harder than flint, I have made your forehead; do not be afraid of them, nor be dismayed at their looks, though they are a rebellious house. . . . Son of man, receive into your heart all My words that I speak to you, and hear with your ears. And go, get to the captives, to the children of your people, and speak to them and tell them, "Thus says the Lord God," whether they hear, or whether they refuse.
>
> Ezekiel 3:8–11

With that reminder, I felt renewed confidence in my calling in God. I found strength from it. I felt as though I was fighting for the Kingdom, for the Word of God, and fighting against compromise. After that, I didn't have any problem continuing to insist that some things about the I-Max services change. Eventually, we got a new volunteer coming in to speak as a result, and this brother was on fire. He was awesome! His name was Reverend Jenkins, and he was a word of faith man who preached the Gospel. He also had a couple guys who would come fill in for him on occasion, and they were all awesome and anointed. It was a great change—and much needed.

We also changed the worship dynamic of the I-Max church. We went from singing all old hymns to singing some worship choruses. I have nothing against old hymns; I love some of the great hymns of the Church. But we needed to add a dynamic element to the I-Max worship, and the more modern choruses accomplished that.

Then the chaplain put me in charge of speaking one Sunday a month. In fact, I was in charge of the whole service on that Sunday. It was my first experience in a lay leadership role. That was the time and place where God began to teach me some basic leadership lessons. I learned so much about how to operate in the giftings that He had given me, and I learned how to flow with His anointing.

I began to live for Sundays at I-Max. My weekdays would be spent in preparation for Sunday. I would prepare messages and read and study and listen to worship music and read and study and prepare messages. I didn't write my messages down or use sermon notes. I would get a message down in my heart, in my spirit, and then I would go from one Scripture to the next. The Scriptures I would write down, one Scripture under the next. I'd do a "Romans road" method with those Scriptures through my whole message, and I'd preach the rest freestyle. I was happy to see the services grow from just 4 to 5 in attendance to almost full, which was 45 to 50 inmates!

Bringing It Home

Later, I got a job working as the warden's porter. Porters cleaned the floors, emptied the trash, vacuumed the offices, cleaned windows, and ran errands for the warden. It turned out I was really good at waxing floors. They would wax floors at night on third shift, when there wasn't as much traffic up through the main entrance at the front of the prison. A porter asked me to help him with the floors one time, so I went up there and did the floors third shift. The next day, the warden came in and went to step on the floors, and he kind of drew back. He asked, "Who left these floors wet?"

The officer with him said, "They're not wet, sir. They're dry."

The warden walked on them and couldn't believe the shine. He asked, "Who did these floors?"

"Benson did," the officer told him.

"Get him up here!" the warden ordered.

I was taken to see him, and the warden told me he wanted me working up there all the time. They switched my job from a regular custodian in the units to a control center area porter. (That was my fancy official designation.) I found a lot of favor in my new job, and I got to know one of the inspectors pretty well. This inspector liked me, so I asked him a favor. I knew that when they did the I-Max services, they recorded them so they could go over the content before playing them back for the level 5 population. I asked him, "Would it be possible to have a couple copies if I bought the tapes? If I have my people bring the tapes in, could I get a couple copies of those messages I've done so I could send them home?"

He agreed to make copies for me, and he said I didn't even have to supply any tapes. He copied two of my favorite messages that I preached and I sent them home, which is a blessing because I still have them to this day. I realize now that those two tapes show the fruit of my "extra" two years of incarceration. God used those two years to train me for the ministry, which is a testament to His timing. I must say, His timing is always better than mine!

13

New Life, New Wife

In prison special times don't come around very often, so when they do, they're all the more important to you. One of those special times is visiting day, when you can have visitors from the outside world. Friends or family may come, or if you're married, your spouse may come and even bring the kids. I didn't have a wife to come see me while I was in prison, but I actually did meet my wife, Stefanie, while I was incarcerated. She came to see me as a visitor. That's one day I will never forget!

Prisoners were allowed a certain number of visits per month, and you could meet your visitors in a special visiting room. People who came to see you would fill out a Visitor Request form and sign it, and they'd usually get coins for the vending machines. That was a great part of visits—you got vending machine food. You could eat all the food your people brought in money for. They'd call you from the unit and say you had a visitor, and then you'd have a certain amount of time to get dressed and get up to the visiting room. Back in those days, you could wear regular street clothes for visits. (Now prisoners have to stay in their "blues.") You could order clothes from the JCPenney catalog, or you could have your people bring you pants and nice shirts and stuff. Visiting days were a time for prisoners to dress up.

Visiting days were one of the very few ways a male prisoner could meet with a woman. Of course, my mom would come up to see me from time to time, and so would my sisters. The other ways we had contact with our families and friends were through mail and collect phone calls. You could only call home if somebody would accept the collect call, and for me, that process is what led to meeting my wife. At the time of my incarceration, my sister Alicia lived in Kentwood in a fourplex, which meant there were four apartments in the same building. She became friends with a young lady named Stefanie who lived underneath her.

As they got to be close friends, my sister found out that Stefanie worked in downtown Grand Rapids for a ministry called Servants Center, which helped take care of the mentally ill and homeless in the city's downtown area. As my sister learned more about the ministry, she got to talking to Stefanie about me.

Being the matchmaker that she is, my sister told Stefanie, "Hey, maybe when my brother, Mike, gets out of prison, he'd be a good volunteer for you. He's a preacher, a minister, and he's going to get out soon. He would be a good person to have down there at Servants Center working with you."

She started dialoging with Stefanie about me, and before long, when my sister would be talking to me on the phone, she would say, "Hang on a second!" Then she would run to Stefanie's apartment and get her to come talk to me on the phone. So Stefanie and I first met by talking to each other on my sister's phone. We started writing letters back and forth, too, and then Stefanie decided she would come visit me in prison.

The day Stefanie was coming to meet me for the first time, I kept looking at the clock every minute that went by. She had said she would be there right on time, at 2:00. About four minutes after 2:00, I started going crazy, afraid she wouldn't make it. Finally, they called my name: "Benson, you have a visitor."

I got all dressed up in my shiny, silvery shirt with short sleeves to show my bulging biceps. Then I went on out to the visiting room, and when Stefanie came through and I laid my eyes on her for the first time, I really did go crazy. All I could see were her gorgeous, beautiful brown eyes. She was (and is) amazing.

As soon as I saw her, I heard the Lord say in my spirit, "That's your wife."

Inwardly, I high-fived myself. All I could think was, *Yes, yes, yes, yes, yes!*

We sat down, and I could tell Stefanie was really nervous. I couldn't blame her, meeting her friend's brother for the first time in the visiting room of a prison. Thinking it would calm her down, I put my hand out, offering to take her hand in mine, and we held hands and had an awesome visit. It was fantastic. In fact, it went so well that after the visit, I made the mistake of writing her the infamous *Hee Haw* letter. This young lady had only met me once, and I was a prisoner. She had never been to a prison before, had never been in trouble in her life, and then she met me through a phone conversation and letters. Next, she met me in person the only way she could—by coming to visit me in prison. In return, I wrote her a letter telling her that God said she was going to be my wife.

Can you imagine that? And after I was done reading the letter I got back from her, I felt like jumping off my bunk, and not with joy. She told me I was going a little too fast for her by talking about marriage after we had only met one time. I was sure I had messed up our relationship already. As soon as I read her letter, I pictured my head turning into a donkey head—like on Bugs Bunny cartoons where Elmer Fudd would get duped by Bugs Bunny, and he'd turn and look at the audience and his head would morph into a donkey head. That's how I felt, like braying *hee-haw, hee-haw.*

In or Out?

Stefanie kept coming to see me, though, and as she and I began to write more letters back and forth and have more visits, we slowly started to fall in love with each other. I was nearing the end of the continuance of my 24-month flop, and it was time for me to go before the parole board for a hearing. Stefanie and I were excited about it because we were making plans for the future. We were sure I was going to get out on parole. I was a role model prisoner, after all, and I worked for the warden. I also had the captain of the corrections officers write me a recommendation, which never happens. To get a corrections officer to write you a recommendation would be one thing all by itself, but to get a captain to write a recommendation for the parole board was unheard of. I had nothing but good work reports, and I had no misconducts. Everything looked great for me to get out.

I went to the interview, and the guy asked me some questions. The way it worked was that one parole board member would vote without seeing me, based on what was in my file, and another would interview me in person. Then they would discuss their votes with each other and with a third board member, and I would need two out of three votes to be granted parole. My interviewer that day was very cordial, and I took that as a positive sign. Then I had to wait for the final decision to come from Lansing, and I was counting the days. I kept asking the counselor all the time if the mail had come in, and if any news had come back for me.

One day the counselor came to me and said, "We got some decisions back. You can go into my office for privacy. Yours is on the desk."

She let me in her office, and I went over to her desk and looked at my paper. It said "Continuance for 12 Months." For just a moment when I first read it, I felt defeated. I got angry and frustrated, but then instantly, the Spirit of God within me welled up and I knew it would be okay. I prayed right there, "God, I don't understand why things have gone this way, but it doesn't matter. Your will be done. I'm going to love You through this, and I'm going to continue to serve You. This is just another year I can spend witnessing to other people. There must be an assignment You have for me in here. There must be more people You need me to reach in here, Lord."

The first person I called when I walked out of that office was Stefanie. I gave her the news, and she took it hard. She was pretty upset. We were all pretty upset, my family and I. But I had already learned that my life was in God's hands, and things happened for a reason. There are times and there are seasons with God for things to happen, and there are purposes He has in mind. So I resigned myself to another 12 months in the I-Max and let it go at that.

Thankfully, that year passed by relatively fast, and I soon found myself preparing for another parole board hearing. The parole board member and my counselor were there, and my sister Alicia had come as a family representative. This time, the interview was drastically different from the first time. This time, there was nothing cordial, nice, or accommodating about the parole board member who questioned me. He was giving me the business, the third degree. He was going over my crimes and saying, "Why should we even let somebody like you out? Look at all the felonies you've committed! You got away with this and that. . . I can't believe this and that . . ."

He just went on and on in that tone. By all appearances, it was the worst interview ever. If anybody had walked in on that interview, judging by what they saw and heard they would have concluded that there was no way I'd get another 12-month continuance. It would be at least 24 months, because the state could give me as many years as it wanted to, a year or two at a time, all the way up to twenty. This guy was acting as though he thought I should serve all my time and then some!

My head was reeling when I walked out of that interview, but something else was in my heart. It was that peace that surpasses all understanding, which guards your heart and mind through Christ

Jesus. (You can read more about that in Philippians chapter 4 in the Bible.) It was almost a month and a half before the final paper came back. Amazingly, I got the news I had been waiting on for so many years. This time, my paper read "P61," the code for parole. I was to be free!

A Very, Very Good Day

I was transferred to a level 1 facility to await my release. It was the first time I'd ever been in a level 1. I was there for two months before my day of freedom arrived. I was to get out on October 31, 2002, right on Halloween. I remember sitting up front that day, waiting for my family to come get me. I was nervous and apprehensive, and so many things were running through my head. I thought about the years I had lost being in prison, and how all my peers would have gone ahead of me in their careers and families by now. I wondered what I would do, how I would find work and what life would be like. Then my family showed up, and it was time for me to leave. A little over six years after the day I gave my heart to Christ, I walked out of prison for the last time.

As I stepped over the threshold of the prison door, the word of the Lord came to me, and He said, "I will restore the years the locusts have eaten out of your life." That was a reference to chapter 2 of the book of Joel in the Old Testament, where God told His people to rejoice because He was going to restore all their losses and take away their shame. It was exactly what I needed to hear.

My first day out was an awesome day. My family was with me, along with Stefanie. We went downtown to see my parole officer, and then we went to Sundance Grill to have breakfast. Boy, did I ever have a breakfast! And I didn't stop there. That night, we went out as a family to Logan's Steak House, and I had the biggest, fattest, juiciest steak I could lay my hands on. It was a very, very good day. It was a day that the Lord had made, and I was rejoicing and being glad in it. I will never forget the joy I felt.

Now that I was free from prison, I had a lot of things to sort out in my mind. The first order of business was getting a job. I went into that process with a lot of false expectations. I guess I thought I'd walk out of prison and God would send some charismatic believer's limousine to pick me up. I'd then be whisked off into a pulpit ministry where I'd be speaking all over the country and all over the world. It didn't turn out quite like that. I had to start out looking for work. Believe me, nobody arrived on my doorstep to whisk me away into a super successful life. I had to work at everything every step of the way.

"Will You Marry Me?"

On top of everything else, there was the whole thing of hoping to get married. Stefanie and I were engaged shortly after I got out. I got her a ring, got on my knee, and asked, "Will you marry me?"

Stefanie said yes, of course. Then I had to meet her dad. Her mom had come to visit me in prison several times, and we had gotten very tight. In fact, now her mother works for our ministry, the Conquerors. But after my release, I still had to meet her dad. I also had to meet her family, who lived out in Midland. You can imagine how nervous I was at those meetings, but I had already expected that I would need to prove myself to a lot of people, and I knew it would not be easy. Stefanie's dad was very cordial, though, right from the start, and over time I won his trust. Now he is like a father to me, not an in-law.

Eight months after my release, Stephanie and I became husband and wife. Trust me, that eight months seemed like a longer wait than any of the time I served in prison. This was a first for me, waiting. All I had known in my past were unhealthy relationships with women, but Stefanie and I wanted to honor the Lord and our marriage covenant by holding off on having sex until we were married. We had both been used to doing things the wrong way in our pasts, and we were determined that we would start our life together by doing things God's way this time around.

In May, we had a beautiful wedding. I was wearing my tux and she was in her dress, and it was gorgeous. We had to honeymoon in Michigan because due to my parole, I was not allowed to leave the state. But that worked out fine. We went to a magnificent Bed & Breakfast place in South Haven, a little town located on the shores of Lake Michigan

After the honeymoon was over, we faced a lot of trials and tribulations together in the first couple years I was out, but we had each other and the Lord. That made all the difference.

14

Captain Conqueror

Even with my criminal record, I did manage to land some jobs eventually. Most places turned me down due to my criminal record, but as people got to know me, they would put in a good word for me in different places. I went from a roofing job to a welding job to a gutter job, and I did the best I could at them. I couldn't stand the time I was spending in that kind of work, though, because all I could think about was, *Where's my life going in this line of work? Where's my calling to preach the Gospel? What happened to all that?*

At the time, we were attending a popular church in Grandville, Michigan. Stefanie, my sister and my family were all heavily invested there. Their hearts were there, and I was all right going there, too, until one day when I was watching Christian programs on TV. I heard this minister named Duane Vander Klok preaching on a show called *Walking by Faith.* At the end of the program, they gave the address of his church: "Resurrection Life Church, 1500 Ivanrest Avenue, Grandville, Michigan."

I immediately thought, *Whoa, wait a minute, I used to live on Ivanrest when I was a kid. I didn't know there was a church there!* I drove on over to that area, and sure enough, there it was, Resurrection Life Church (RLC). It was quite large. The pastor's TV message had grabbed my attention and touched me, and I told Stephanie I wanted to check the place out. I went to a Wednesday night service, but Pastor Duane wasn't speaking that night; it was another pastor. As I walked into the sanctuary for the first time, however—as soon as I walked in—the Lord spoke to me. He said, "This is your home. One day you'll speak here."

I brought Stefanie to RLC not long after that, and we started attending there regularly. Eventually my sister and family also made the switch, and we were all at one church again, which was great. I started going to the men's breakfast every Tuesday morning, and it wasn't long before I got plugged in and served wherever I could at RLC. I still couldn't stand the jobs I was working at, but the Lord was teaching me through them. He was grooming me. I had thought I was ready to enter the ministry, but He told me, "No, you're not ready." He kept preparing me in His way, in His time. On my side I was getting a little impatient with the process, so one day I had it out with Him while I was working my gutter job. I argued a little bit that I had done a lot more ministry in prison, and that He should have me working in ministry now, not these other jobs.

The Lord's answer stopped me in my tracks. He said, "If you treat *this* job as though it's your ministry, then you'll move into true ministry."

In my head and in my flesh, I still did not like the work I was doing, but in my heart I finally got to a place of contentment. "Godliness with contentment is great gain," Scripture says in 1 Timothy 6:6. My heart was finally content with the work I was doing. I was also content to serve in whatever ways I could at RLC. I knew that God would move me into whatever ministry He wanted me to do, so long as I was faithful where I was at now. I have always said that you'll gravitate toward where God wants you to be positioned in the Body of Christ. You don't have to strive to get there or let everybody know where they *should* put you. My philosophy is that if you just follow the Lord and stay faithful, you'll gravitate to where you belong in the Kingdom.

So many people are striving to be somebody God has not called them to be in the Church. They chase after a position instead of after God. So many people want to be a preacher or a pastor or a this or a that, but you rarely see anybody excited about filling the behind-the-scenes positions: "Man, I get to serve in the administrative office," or "Wow, I get to serve in the Helps Ministry," or "Hey, I get to serve as a volunteer who prays for people." Everybody wants the big, glitzy positions. But you don't have to be placed out front as soon as you walk in. You don't have to arrive and say, "I'm called to be this... I'm a leader. . . put me here or there." You just go out and serve, and God will make it evident what He's called you to be. Then He'll take care of putting you there. In His time He'll appoint you and give you favor, and people will discern in their spirit what it is you are called to do. That's the position God has ordained for you.

A Tempting Alternative

After Stephanie and I became members at RLC, I decided to sign up for Bible school. I enrolled in the Christian Life School of Theology the church offered. I learned a lot and became even closer to the Lord. It was during that year that a distraction from the enemy came my way. The enemy knew how much I hated my job, and he offered me a tempting alternative. This became another testing time in my life. Would I wait on the Lord for His timing, or would I take matters into my own hands? (When people say they take matters into their own hands, that's just another way of saying they're following the ways of the world or the god of this world, god with a small *g*—Satan.)

Satan offered me a tempting alternative to waiting on the Lord. At that time, Alicia's mother-in-law worked for one of the premier realtors in all of Grand Rapids, Green Ridge Realty. This lady had connections and could get me into the company under her son, my brother-in-law. He would train me, and I would take the test and get my realtor's license and everything. It sounded like a fantastic opportunity, and I was excited by it. The real estate market was doing really well back then, and I already knew I had a gift in the area of sales. I could sell things to people so easily. Some people even told me I could sell ice cubes to Eskimos. It was a natural gifting or talent God had placed in me. I started thinking about all the money I could make in real estate. I started thinking about how I could set my own hours and not have a boss telling me every move to make. I started thinking about how I could dress nicely and drive a nice car. *Life would be perfect if only I could get my real estate license and start selling real estate,* my mind told me.

I was more than ready to try something new. I was excited about making the change. There was only one hitch—my wife wasn't in agreement with it.

"I'm not feeling this, Mike," Stefanie told me. "I don't think this is from God."

I got attitude when she said that. "What are you talking about? This is clearly from God!" I told her. "And you know how much I love the job I'm at now," I added sarcastically.

Our conversations got pretty intense, and we had a lot of angst between us over this decision. Frustrated, one day I went into the bathroom at work and had it out with the Lord (again). I said, "God, what's up with this? What's going on with this? How come Stefanie isn't getting it? How come I'm feeling this way? This change is supposed to be a good thing. How come I'm so frustrated?"

God answered me very cleanly and clearly. He said, "I have not delivered you from prison and given you your freedom so that you could be a welder, a roofer or a real estate salesman. *I freed you to preach the Gospel.* That's what you are. I made you to preach the Gospel."

That settled it for me. "Okay, Lord," I said.

I walked out of the bathroom and called my wife. "You're right," I told her. "God just spoke to me, and I turned down my position at the real estate school."

That was a key decision in my life, another testing time in my journey with following the Lord Jesus Christ. Life is full of tests and trials, learning experiences and opportunities. The important thing in those times is hearing God's voice and following His path for you.

A New "Baby"

I really liked attending the men's breakfast at RLC, which is called Iron Sharpens Iron, from Proverbs 27:17: "Iron sharpens iron, so one man sharpens another" (NASB). This group of men gets together each Tuesday morning for breakfast. A speaker comes in and gives a message, and we discuss it afterward. I found it a very good, encouraging ministry that helped me grow.

One morning, the guest speaker was a man named James DeMelo. He had been a well-known bodybuilder back in the 1980s. He appeared on the cover of a lot of sport magazines. Now James was an evangelist, and he was also the founder of a team called the Conquerors International Strength Team. This group of athletes, the Conquerors, travels all over the United States and all over the world and uses feats of strength to captivate audiences and deliver the Gospel message.

I met some people who knew James at that breakfast when he was speaking, so I got to talk to him afterward. He asked me if I had spoken to Greg Molchan. I said I knew who Greg was; he was in my Bible school class at the church. Greg came up just then, and we all talked some more.

After a little conversation, James said to me, "You should consider joining the Conquerors."

"What is it? What do you do?" I asked.

They filled me in. Greg and I decided that we would meet up and I would go with him to a couple Conquerors events to see what it was all about. The first time I went to a Conquerors event, I knew immediately that it was something God was calling me to. There was no doubt in my mind. Ever since I was a little boy, I had lifted weights. I had followed Arnold Schwarzenegger and other bodybuilders. My whole time in prison, I had spent time amassing quite a physique. I had a lot of strength and muscle size. The idea of doing feats of strength that led up to an opportunity to preach the Gospel really appealed to me. They didn't have to ask me twice to join the team.

Joining the Conquerors was exciting for me. There would be days when I would go out in the driveway of our duplex and practice tearing decks of cards in half in my hand. I would practice tearing phone books in half and busting sealed pop cans in my grip and bending horseshoes and steel bars and all the crazy stuff that we do on the team. Being out in the driveway, at least I didn't make a mess of our place inside.

Greg was running the Conquerors team for James at the time. James was acting as the president of the board and the head of the ministry. Then Greg announced that he was leaving the Conquerors to become a youth pastor. That left James looking for a new team captain. I had joined the team without having much leadership or ministry experience other than in prison, yet James looked my way when he needed a new captain.

When James approached me, he put it this way to me: "I'm going to give you my baby."

I wondered to myself, *Hmm, what does that mean?*

I soon found out. James had his office in the bottom of his house in Byron Center. He had me over for a board meeting one day. At that meeting, he signed over the whole Conquerors ministry to me—his baby. It was precious to him, and he stayed on the board as founder. But within six months' time, I became the new head of the Conquerors International Strength Team.

I joined the Conquerors in 2004, and I took it over in 2005. I started off by moving the Conquerors office into my basement. And I prayed, "Lord, show me what to do about this ministry."

The Lord answered by giving me a gardening illustration. He said, "The first year, the ministry will sleep. The second year, the ministry will creep. And the third year, the ministry will leap."

That answer really encouraged me, and I needed a lot of encouragement that first year. It was challenging, but Stefanie and I learned a lot and grew a lot during that time.

A Leap of Faith

The ministry may have been sleeping that first year, but our learning curve was leaping! Stephanie was still working for Servants Center downtown, and I was still working at my gutter job. Our first child, Sofia, had just been born, and Stefanie was on maternity leave when we both got a word from the Lord that we were to quit our jobs and go into full-time ministry. This was a huge, *huge* leap of faith, especially financially. Stefanie's job was bringing in the most money, but even with my income added to hers, we were barely paying the bills.

We decided to step out in faith anyway. We stepped out into full-time ministry with the Conquerors International Strength Team. What a season of testing that leap of faith began for us. It seemed as though the Lord was bringing us through many seasons of testing in preparation for what lay ahead. He did a lot of pruning in us. He pruned off the things that were dead so that He could make way for the life that He wanted to live through us.

It was not an easy process. One time, we wound up two months behind on our mortgage payments. We had just purchased the house that same year, 2005, and now we were about to be foreclosed on. All our other bills were adding up, too. We had a whole seventy-five cents in our bank account.

Understandably, my wife became upset, which upset me. I went in the bathroom one day feeling so tempted to shake my fist at God. My flesh was pressing me hard to rant and rave and cry out, "Why,

God?" But my spirit rose up within me, and I offered Him a prayer of thanksgiving instead. Then I went out and took Stefanie by the hand, and I began to pray. We both began to shed tears of joy because God's presence filled the room as He began to comfort and exhort us.

No sooner did we finish the session with our Father when the doorbell rang. I ran upstairs and answered the door. This guy I knew, who held a checkbook in his hand, was standing there.

Right away, he said, "Mike, let me in. I've got to do this quickly."

He rushed in, sat down and wrote four checks for a thousand dollars each, for a total of four thousand dollars. God had moved through this brother in the Lord, and his obedience brought provision to our household. It was the supernatural provision of the Lord, and it was just amazing. Since then, Stefanie and I have been blessed to see God move in that way many, many times over throughout our years of ministry.

Standing on Faith

That year of 2005 also brought my first missions trip overseas, to Rio de Janeiro, Brazil. The Conquerors were going to Brazil as part of James DeMelo's crusade there. It would be my first missions trip as the captain of the Conquerors, and as the executive director and president of the ministry. But for a while, I was concerned it wouldn't happen. That's when I learned another lesson about standing on my faith.

About three months prior to our planned trip, Greg and I were doing a summer outreach at the Resurrection Life Church in Muskegon (there are many Resurrection Life Church International churches all over the country and the world). One of our feats of strength involves taking a five-eighths-inch steel bar and bending it over our skull or around our neck into the shape of a U. Then we twist the bar, grab it and cross it over into the shape of fish. We can also bend it under our leg, under our thigh, or in our teeth. That day

I was feeling frisky, and I made the classic mistake of not warming up. I bent one bar and said, "Yeah, I'm going to go for it. I'm going to bend two steel bars taped together."

I attempted the two five-eighths-inch steel bars taped together. These are world strongman qualifying steel bars. That means people who compete in the World's Strongest Man competition that you see on ESPN have to bend one of these steel bars around the back of their neck first just to qualify for the competition. So we're talking a world-class level feat of strength just to bend one bar, and I had taped two of them together. I went under my leg and tried bending them, and I was doing pretty well. Then I heard a *snap* in my right arm.

Right away, I knew something had gone drastically wrong. I knew I had injured myself, but I didn't know how severely. Come to find out that I had torn my right bicep. Usually that's a bad injury. I remember thinking to myself, *Oh no, how am I going to be able to do any feats of strength, let alone do anything, while leading this team in Rio de Janeiro?*

The trip was scheduled, and I needed to go. I knew in my spirit what I needed to do. I had to stand on my faith and believe God for a miracle. All the way up until the trip, I was confessing the Word of God over my injury, saying, "By His stripes I'm healed." (See 1 Peter 2:24 and Isaiah 53:5.) I was in terrible pain. My arm hurt all the time. I wouldn't go to a doctor, however, because I didn't want to hear a bad report. I wanted to stay in faith, so I kept confessing my healing and standing on the Word for the healing.

My arm was still hurting when we boarded the plane for Rio de Janeiro. In our first performance during the crusade, one of the team members had the steel bar in his hand, ready to give it to me, and he said to me, "Do you want me to have somebody else bend it?"

"No," I said, "healed men do not shy away from a steel bar."

I took the steel bar and bent it over my head. It was at that moment, when I bent the steel bar over my head, that God supernaturally healed my right bicep. I didn't even notice it at the time, really, but I did notice that from that moment on, there was no pain. My strength wasn't limited in any way. I had received an awesome miracle from the Lord. That crusade was just the first of many international missions trips that I would oversee as captain of the Conquerors International Strength Team.

15

Transforming the World

The Conquerors International Strength Team exists to transform communities worldwide with the Gospel of Jesus Christ. The Conquerors accomplish this mission and vision by bringing communities together for a strength team performance in which our team members do many different feats of strength, and then we deliver the Gospel to our audience. We've seen literally hundreds of thousands of people come to know the Lord Jesus Christ through our community outreach events.

Typically, a church invites us into a city, and we go in and start with performances in the public schools. Those are a rallying point for any community, something that gets the whole community together. Our school assemblies work really well because whatever walk of life people come from, they typically will get behind anything that will positively benefit the children of the community. A large part of our ministry involves these school assemblies.

First, we go into an area's schools and deliver a totally secular motivational message. We tailor that message to fit that area's needs. The kids may need to hear an anti-bullying message, or an anti-drug message, or they may some encouragement about doing their best, excelling at what they do, and resisting peer pressure. We can tailor our message around whatever subjects school officials suggest. We go in and do a school assembly in front of the students. We blow up hot water bottles, and we do things like calling students forward to test out the metal horseshoes before we bend them. We include all kinds of interaction with the students. Everywhere we go, the kids absolutely love it.

The team's feats of strength captivate the kids' attention, and then we invite them back for more. We say, "Hey, if you thought this was awesome, if you thought this was great, wait until you see us tonight at (so-and-so) Church. Meet us there at (whatever time) to see us break bricks with our arms, our elbows, and our heads! We'll even light some bricks on fire! It's going to be awesome, so come and bring your family and friends."

We create quite a buzz within the community because the students go home and tell everyone all about what they saw at the assembly, and they want to come back for more. That's always our hope—that many of the students who get a taste of our feats of strength at school will want to come back to see the "big show" after school. The elementary-aged kids especially want to come back to our evening events, and the only way they can come is to bring their moms and dads as their drivers.

Then in the evening we have a community-wide event—the big show—either at the church that brought us in or at a neutral location if an association of churches is participating. It is always great when churches join together to bring us into the community to do an outreach. Sometimes, we might do our event at the local high school after hours. Wherever it takes place, at that event we usually see literally hundreds of people come forward in the altar call. We've often had whole families—Dad, Mom, and all the kids—up at the altar call giving their hearts to the Lord Jesus Christ. After the event, we connect the people who came forward with one of the local churches that hosted us. We let the churches disciple these new believers afterward and become their new spiritual family.

We have done thousands of these community outreach events all over the United States. I can't tell you the countless times we've seen God do miraculous things. We've seen people healed. We've seen people delivered from demonic oppression and possession. We've seen people baptized and filled with the Holy Spirit. We've seen whole communities come together and receive healing through the anointing of the Lord Jesus Christ. Nothing is more exciting for us than to have God's power and presence flow over to touch the people who come to see our events.

Getting Hope into the Schools

When I first joined the Conquerors and then took it over in 2005, I was introduced to a ministry called One Hope. One Hope is responsible for creating the *Book of Hope*, a Scripture book designed to engage children and young people in various cultures and show them God's redemptive plan through Jesus' life, death, and resurrection. The book is a harmonized version of the Gospels, so to speak, chronologically ordered and put into different editions for different age groups, cultures, and circumstances.

One Hope is literally reaching millions of young people all over the planet with the Gospel as presented in the *Book of Hope*. Now One Hope has also put out a video, *The GodMan*, and even an app for iPhones and smartphones. The whole ministry of One Hope is amazing. It has been one of our ministry's key strategic partners because it has given us a tool that reaches young people with the Gospel even in a public school setting. The Conquerors are even more effective through strategic partnerships with ministries like One Hope that are bigger than we are. We work really well together to spread the Gospel. With One Hope, in fact, now we even have a Conquerors edition of the *Book of Hope* that we can give out at our assemblies. We continue to love our partnership with One Hope!

How do we go about getting God's Word into public schools? It's simple: We go into a public school and have an interview with the principal. We show him or her a video of our assemblies, and we provide recommendations from principals of other schools we've visited. We also say we have a gift we'd like to offer to students, and it's called the *Book of Hope*. We bring the book with us to the interview so the principal can review it. We explain that for high school and middle school assemblies, we hold up the *Book of Hope* and let the students know that it's a free gift, but that it does have Christian content. We explain how we let the students make the choice. We let them know that the books are on tables at the doorways, and if they want one, they can take one, but if they don't, that's fine, too. The choice is entirely up to the students. Often, a principal will say yes to our *Book of Hope* distribution on those terms. If he or she wants to say no, we stress that there's no problem; we just won't set up the *Book of Hope* distribution at that school.

With elementary students, we use a different format. We tell the principal about the *Book of Hope*, and then we provide a letter the principal can send home with the students prior to our visit. The letter informs parents that there will be a Conqueror assembly on such-and-such date at the school, and that there will be a free gift made available for the children. The letter says that the gift is a booklet that does have Christian content, so the parents need to sign yes or no on the letter and send it back to the school to indicate whether their child may bring home a booklet. This format has worked well for getting the Gospel into the hands of the younger students.

We also have a partnership with an organization called the West Michigan Kingdom Coalition, which is a group of business people who sponsor and fund evangelistic ministries and efforts that originate here in West Michigan. Through their sponsorship, we are able to offer our school assemblies without a fee, or at a reduced fee, if the schools are agreeable to the *Book of Hope* being offered to the student body as a gift. This coalition is directly funding the distribution of the Word of God to students across America!

The public school system is one of the hardest places in America to get the Gospel into, but so far, between our distributions in the public schools stateside and our overseas missions trips, we have handed out close to one million of these *Book of Hope* booklets! This is nothing compared to what the actual organization, One Hope, distributes. (For more information about One Hope, please visit their webpage at www.onehope.net.) They saturate a whole country in a very short span of time, literally distributing millions and millions of copies. Still, we are really glad to help in every way we can, especially inside America's public schools.

Filipino Miracle

The Conquerors International Strength Team has visited almost thirty different countries around the world to minister the Gospel. We also have been on TV in front of a national audience on Sky Angel Christian television, and I have personally appeared on the TBN and TCT networks to share my testimony about God's redeeming power in the life of a former prisoner.

The Conquerors have been to the Philippines three times. We work with the Church Multiplication Coalition there, headed up under Pastor Jill Boyonas. It's a dynamic ministry with a very big vision for Philippines, and that's to reach all of the Philippines with the Gospel of Jesus Christ. We go into these barangays, or villages, with a crusade format and do skits and dramas, and then one or more of us will perform feats of strength and minister the Gospel.

On one trip to the Philippines (I think it was our first one), we had just spent ten days ministering to crowds of hundreds and sometimes thousands of people. When we gave an altar call, many of them had reached out their hands and come forward. We had lined them up and started praying for the sick, and people were getting healed and delivered from demons all over the place. People were getting baptized and filled with the Holy Spirit. God's miracles were abundant.

After ten days of this, we were back in the big city of Manila, feeling tired and worn out. I was with a good friend and partner of many years, Larry Martin, and a fellow evangelist, Clint Herrema. We had spent those ten days eating rice, kemilau, balut, and all these other Filipino dishes, so we were on the lookout for some American food. We were so excited to find a Chili's restaurant. We were sitting there in Chili's, enjoying our food, when we noticed an Indian man at the bar. He was with a young Filipino lady who seemed very intoxicated. The next thing I knew, Clint was over there talking to this man at the bar. I didn't pay that much attention to them since I was busy chowing down my Mango shake and other food, but then Larry tapped me on the shoulder and told me to check out what Clint was up to.

It turned out that the man's leg was in some sort of brace. The leg was probably six or seven inches shorter than the other leg, and it was twisted. He had been run over by a car in his youth, and the accident had maimed his leg. He had been crippled ever since. Clint had the brace off the leg, and he was taking off the guy's shoe, which had an extended heel. Pretty soon Clint had the guy's bare foot in his hand.

The guy was kind of laughing at what Clint was doing, probably embarrassed, but Clint went ahead and prayed for him right there at the bar, in front of everybody. And right there in public, the guy's leg straightened out and grew to a length that matched his other leg!

Instantly, the guy sobered up. He started jumping up and down and kissing Clint on the head. He was ecstatic. The Lord had done a miracle right there in Chili's! Then Clint brought the man to our table and turned him over to me.

The man sat down and introduced himself and said, "I am Hindu."

I was thinking to myself, *Oh man, okay, I am so tired, but look what just happened . . . praise God!* As weary as I was, the Holy Spirit rose up in me, and I looked him straight in the eyes and said, "Sir, how long have you been like this with your leg?"

"Since I was a young boy," he answered.

I said, "Sir, have there been Hindu prayers prayed over you for your leg?"

"Yes, many times," he answered.

I said, "Sir, the reason those prayers didn't work is because those gods you worship in Hinduism are not really gods at all. The reason your leg is straight now is because of the name above every name, the name of Jesus Christ. And this Jesus, the Son of the living God, didn't die only so we could perform miracles in His name. He died so we could perform the greatest miracle—introducing you to Him and letting Him do a miracle in your heart. Do you believe that?"

He looked at me and shook his head yes, so I led him in the sinner's prayer right there at the dinner table in Chili's.

I noticed there was an Australian man at the bar who had been watching us and had witnessed everything. I had already eaten and I was full, so I figured, *Well, we might as well go after him, too.* I went up and started a conversation with him and talked to him for over an hour, but he just denied and denied what he had seen and came up with every excuse for not acknowledging the Lord, who had just done a miracle right in front of his face. I learned a lesson then, that salvation is in the hands of the Lord. There are those who are seeking with their hearts, and then there are those whose hearts are hardened. When people's hearts are turned against God and they don't want anything to do with Him, they are not receptive to the Gospel.

Peru Pandemonium

On another missions trip, we traveled to the nation of Peru. We were working with a very influential church in Lima, and we were going to do a mass evangelism crusade. Conquerors team members Scott Smith and Angela DeGraff (one of our female team members) were with me. Of course, in every country we go to, people want to take us to the gyms. We definitely want to visit the gyms, too, because we need to keep our bodies loose and in shape at all times so we can perform the feats that draw people in so we can preach the Gospel to them. So Scott, Angela, and I went into one gym, and TV news cameras followed us in. It seemed as if we caused pandemonium everywhere we went on that trip.

When we visited the schools, we practically got mobbed. The young people went nuts over these big, strong Americans who included a lady. They couldn't believe it. At one of the girls' schools, Scott and I basically had to hide out in the bus while we let Angela go out and do the Conquerors thing. Those girls were just too crazy; Scott and I could not even make an appearance!

We held the mass crusade in the Rimac district, which is a suburb of Lima. We set it up right in the streets. Tons of pastors were in attendance, all in suits. There was a band. There were TV cameras from three different stations. There were thousands of people who showed up. It was pandemonium again. We performed our feats of strength, and as always, I ministered the Gospel afterward. When it came time to ask people if they wanted to make a decision for the Lord Jesus Christ, we saw thousands of hands go up in the air. It was wild.

After that, we began to pray for the sick. As I looked out into the crowd, I noticed that there was one man who was staring at me intently. It was not a friendly stare. He was moving up in the line, and he kept staring at me as hard as he could. As he got closer, some of the other pastors with us were looking his way because they had noticed him as well.

Something in my spirit told me that this man was not in line for healing. He was in line to spy us out. He was a witch doctor. Finally, he reached the front of the line. I put my hands on his head. He had his face bent toward the ground, but his eyes were still looking up toward me.

I grabbed him and said, "I know who you are, Satan. You get out of here now, in Jesus' name!"

The man's eyes got really wide, and he ran through the crowd as fast as he could to get away from there.

I sat there and laughed—not at the man, of course. I felt bad for him, but I was laughing at the enemy. Satan will try to use any tactic he can to intimidate us. As I saw the man run away, I thought, *Satan, I've spent 11 years in prison. I've had people try to stab me. I've been in unbelievably bloody fights. It's going to take more than a guy staring me down in a crowd to scare me and make me fearful.*

Making New Memories in Pisco

After our crusade in Lima, we traveled several hours north to the coastal city of Pisco. A year previously, Pisco had suffered a massive earthquake in which thousands and thousands of people had perished. The city was still in the process of rebuilding when we arrived. Everywhere we drove, we saw piles of rubble that used to be houses or buildings. Some of these buildings had collapsed with people inside, and work crews could not get the bodies out even a year later. Peru didn't have much in the way of heavy equipment, especially out in the rural areas. The situation caused a putrid smell that I can't even describe. The smell of death was everywhere. In the middle of all that death, we had come to bring Life.

One night we conducted a crusade in the town square, right in the center of town. The pastor we were with explained to me that when the earthquake had occurred, there had been a funeral procession going on at the Catholic church kitty-corner to the same square in which we were standing. Some dignitary had died, and a large procession was entering the church, including mayors and officials. When the earthquake came, the church caved in and killed everyone in attendance, so the town lost much of its leadership and many of its people all at once, right in the very spot where we were. They had stacked literally thousands of bodies in that square afterward. It was where they had collected the dead and tried to identify them.

That night as we were ministering the Gospel, I remember looking out on the crowd of people and thinking about all they had lost and all they had been through. Yet here they were, seeking hope, seeking strength, seeking encouragement. I told them the story of how Jesus came to save the lost and how He came to deliver people from the power of darkness and to take away the sting of death.

Then I asked them at the end, "In this city, when you look at this square, you have images of death in your minds. You see people, your loved ones, who were the victims of a catastrophe. But tonight we're going to erase that memory, and we're going to make a new one. We're going to make a memory of life."

I addressed the people in that city, telling them that death can never overcome life. I told them that life is victorious over death, because Jesus of Nazareth came forth from the tomb. He was raised from the dead on the third day. I told them the power and sting of death have been removed by life through Christ Jesus. Then I asked if anyone present wanted to receive life by accepting Jesus into their heart as their Savior. Five thousand people raised their hands and came forward!

That's the essence of the Gospel—our Savior has overcome death and has restored us to life in Him. So many people in so many countries have gone to church and have experienced a form of religion, but they haven't really experienced the power and life of the Gospel. I believe that when we preach the Gospel from hearts filled with the Holy Spirit, God will confirm His message through signs and wonders. People will be saved. People will be healed and delivered. Alcoholics and drug addicts will be set free in an instant. The lame will walk and the dead will rise, because that is the essence of the Gospel.

The Gospel is so much more than a story about a Man from the past, a religious leader from days gone by. It's not just a story of some kind of cosmic god or something. It is the story of creation. It is the story of life. "In Him was life, and the life was the light of men," says John 1:4. People were meant to experience the Gospel in action and to see the hand of God moving by listening to the Word of God. We definitely saw the hand of God move in Peru. We later found out we had reached millions of people with the Gospel in the few days that we were there through the television outreach and through our crusades and school visits. Countless salvations resulted from that tour. It was a highly successful missions trip.

Costa Rica Wonder

When the Conquerors ministered in Costa Rica, we went into several schools as usual, only in places like Costa Rica, the Philippines, and some countries in South America and Africa, it's much easier to openly share the Gospel in the schools and distribute the *Book of Hope*. We were in a city called Jaco, a resort town where there are a lot of high-end luxury resorts. Jaco is also known for prostitution, which is legal in that country. Driving through the city at night, we passed a little establishment that was supposedly a bar, but was also a whole lot more. At night, taxis would literally line up for blocks in front of the bar, picking up and dropping off johns. Those johns were usually men from the high-end resorts, heading out to get women.

Another pandemic spreading across our planet right now is human trafficking. A lot of human trafficking activity goes through Costa Rica, so we knew going into Jaco that we would be waging war in a place of intense spiritual battle. We went into the schools first, and we found out where we were going to do our crusade that evening. Guess where it was—in a park right next to that questionable establishment! There was big gap between that building and several other buildings on the block. The city had built a huge park in that gap. Literally thousands of people were packed into that little park area to watch us that night.

We got to our evening crusade site, and vendors were set up everywhere selling empanadas and giving away free water. We had our good friends along, James and Vonda Dally, Greg and Leah Molchan, and Wally and June Blume. My wife, Stephanie, was along as well. Greg and I went up and started things off by breaking bricks and bending steel bars. Once again, the Lord moved and showed Himself mighty in a miraculous way. When we gave the altar call, hundreds, if not thousands, of people answered the altar call.

In that moment, a phenomenon took place that several of the people from the United States saw. They said that when we gave the altar call and people's hands were raised up all over, in the center of the crowd above them four big birds appeared in the sky and formed a triangle. To give you a visual, the bird at the top point of the triangle had a second bird right behind it, and the others were to the left and to the right, forming the triangle. The people who witnessed it were amazed because none of these birds flew in; they just appeared there and hovered in a triangle, and then they all flew off in different directions. I didn't see it myself; I was too focused on the crowd at the time. But it was just another sign or wonder from the Lord.

One of the greatest reports of all that night was that it was one of the first nights ever that the little bar we were next to had no business. No taxis lined up to facilitate the prostitution business. We literally shut the devil's door that night.

Another great report involved the healings that took place that night. We saw several people healed at that crusade. A young man was there whose Achilles tendons were shorter than they were supposed to be. He had to walk around on his tiptoes all the time. He was instantly healed, and he was able to put his heels down on the ground for the first time in many years and walk around normally. It was fantastic, and it was only one of the many, many miracles that took place. The hand of God moved powerfully in that place to save and to heal. He destroyed the works of darkness and defeated the enemy, Satan.

Our Approach to Ministry

We see the ministry of the Conquerors as a spiritual battle because it is one. When we go into a city or community, we got to war. We go in to push back the kingdom of darkness and to advance the Kingdom of God. We expect to stand our ground, and we expect to take new ground as the Light of Christ overwhelms the darkness. Everywhere we have gone, we have been able to say with 2 Corinthians 2:14, "Thanks be to God, who always leads us in triumph in Christ, and manifests through us the sweet aroma of the knowledge of Him in every place" (NASB).

Going into an area, we bathe ourselves and that community in prayer. We take authority over the powers, the principalities, and the rulers of dark places that are in charge of that area, and we conduct spiritual warfare through prayer and praying in the Spirit. We loose ministering angels, and we pray for open doors of favor. We literally wreak havoc in the enemy's camp. We send confusion into the camp of the enemy. We are instrumental in destroying his works.

Jesus said it best in John 10:10: "The thief does not come except to steal, and to kill, and to destroy. I have come that they may have life, and that they may have it more abundantly." *That* is the power of the Gospel. It's not just empty words. It's backed up by the power of Heaven. It's not just sermons. It's backed up by the power of the Holy Ghost. It's not just, "Believe me because I'm telling you this." It's God showing Himself strong and mighty.

As the Conquerors International Strength Team, we are so honored that God can use us and the human feats of strength we perform as an entry point to usher in the power and might of His saving message. Each of us on the team is committed to continue doing all we can, in as many places as we can, to transform communities worldwide with the Gospel of Jesus Christ.

His Good Plan

I will never forgot how God has shown Himself strong in my life. Even as a child and a youth, when I didn't know Him and didn't realize He had a good plan for my life, God was there. Even when I was busily engaged in evil, going on crime sprees and running from the law, His mercy and grace were extended toward me and He preserved my life. Even in prison, when it looked as though I would spend long decades of my life incarcerated and when I had given up on myself, God had not given up on me. He had my freedom planned long before I deserved to be free, and He brought me freedom not just on the outside, but on the inside, in my inner man, where I needed Him the most.

Even if I had spent the rest of my life in prison, I would have been free in His love and salvation, but incarceration wasn't His plan for me. He gave me a new life and a new wife and a ministry I never expected, doing the feats of strength that I love and preaching His Word that I have come to love more than anything in this world. He has healed the wounds of my heart that came with my family of origin. With my wife, Stefanie, and our kids Sofia and Ryland, He has given me the family of my own that my heart always desired. And in 2013, as I told you in the very beginning, He restored my health and strength after the debilitating stroke and all its negative effects on me, and now I am back on the road, serving Him and walking in His good plan. He has made me more than a conqueror, and He can and will do the same thing for you. Always keep in mind that you are more than a conqueror through Christ Jesus. Keep in mind this final word from Romans 8:31–49 (NKJV) in God's Word, the Bible:

> If God is for us, who can be against us? He who did not spare His own Son, but delivered Him up for us all, how shall He not with Him also freely give us all things? Who shall bring a charge against God's elect? It is God who justifies. Who is he who condemns?

It is Christ who died, and furthermore is also risen, who is even at the right hand of God, who also makes intercession for us. Who shall separate us from the love of Christ? Shall tribulation, or distress, or persecution, or famine, or nakedness, or peril, or sword? . . .

Yet in all these things we are more than conquerors through Him who loved us. For I am persuaded that neither death nor life, nor angels nor principalities nor powers, nor things present nor things to come, nor height nor depth, nor any other created thing, shall be able to separate us from the love of God which is in Christ Jesus our Lord.

EPILOGUE

A Life-Changing Moment

If you would like to experience the life and freedom that God offers through the sacrifice of His Son, Jesus Christ, then give your heart and life to Him. It is one decision that will change your life forever! You have just read all about how I made that very same decision and how it changed my life in more ways than I could even tell you about in the pages of this book.

Take a moment to pray the following prayer. Say it with your mouth and mean it from your heart, as Romans 10:9–10 (NASB) in the Bible tells us to do, for "if you confess with your mouth Jesus as Lord, and believe in your heart that God raised Him from the dead, you will be saved; for with the heart a person believes, resulting in righteousness, and with the mouth he confesses, resulting in salvation."

Those are some good results! And you can count on God to keep His Word. The very next verse in that Scripture also tells us about another good result. It says, "Whoever believes on Him will not be put to shame" (Romans 10:11 NKJV). Another translation puts it this way: "Whoever believes in Him will not be disappointed" (NASB). I experienced plenty of shame and disappointment in my life before I asked Jesus to be my Lord—shame in myself and disappointment in other people and in how my life was going. Once I gave my life to Christ, however, He turned all that around and replaced my shame and disappointment with forgiveness and righteousness in Him, and with a good plan, God's plan, for my life. He can and will do the same for you. You won't believe how good the results are!

Are you ready for a life-changing moment? Pray this prayer right now:

> *Dear Jesus, I ask You to make me new and give me life. I believe that You died for my sins on the cross so that I could have a relationship with Father God. I believe that after three days in the tomb, God raised You from the dead. This day I make You, Jesus, my Lord and Savior, and I commit my life to You. From this day forward, I'm going to live for You; I'm not going to live to please myself any longer. Thank You, Jesus. Amen.*

Congratulations on your new life! Now that Jesus is your Lord and Savior, everything is going to change. It might take a little time—remember that I had to learn about and grow in my new faith, and I didn't get out of jail the instant I accepted Christ either. But He began a process in me that took me off my old path in life and put me on a new path, following His plan instead of my own. It didn't take long for me to find out that His plan was far better!

If you're wondering about what to do next as you start your new life in Christ, visit The Starting Line at my church's www.reslife.org/about-us/the-starting-line/page. It is an online resource my church puts out that will really help you. There is a free downloadable book called *Your New Life* that my pastor, Duane Vander Klok, wrote to help new believers get started growing in their faith. There are also great Bible reading plans you can download and a number to call if you need prayer.

With Jesus as Lord, no matter what your past has been like or what comes your way in the future, you are *more than a conqueror*. Welcome to the family of God!

ABOUT THE AUTHOR

Mike Benson is president and team captain of the Conquerors International Strength Team, a group of athletes who use feats of strength to captivate audiences worldwide and deliver the Gospel of Jesus Christ. Mike is also an evangelist from Resurrection Life Church in Grandville, Michigan. He has ministered to millions of people and has seen over 250,000 make decisions for Christ in the last ten years. A motivational teacher, Mike serves as a certified speaker, trainer, and coach with the John Maxwell Team and has taught in schools, colleges, and companies in many countries, with an emphasis on overcoming life's obstacles and turning adversity into opportunity. Having spent eleven years of his life in prison, Mike also has a heart for those who are incarcerated and has shared his story in thousands of prisons around the world. Mike lives in Jenison, Michigan, with his wife, Stefanie, and their two children.

You can find out more about Mike and his ministry by visiting the Conquerors International Strength Team online at www.theconquerors.net or www.facebook.com/pages/The-Conquerors-Strength-Team/62706772275. Mike would also like to hear from you about how reading this book has ministered to you. You can reach Mike by emailing him through the "Contact" tab on the Conquerors' website.

Printed in the United States
By Bookmasters